Introduction to Artificial Intelligence: Build Your First AI Model with Python

A Step-by-Step Guide to Getting Started with AI and Machine Learning

MIGUEL FARMER

RAFAEL SANDERS

Table of Content

TABLE OF CONTENTS

INTRODUCTION

Learning AI: From Fundamentals to Cutting-Edge Applications

Welcome to *Learning AI: From Fundamentals to Cutting-Edge Applications*. This book is designed to guide you through the fascinating world of Artificial Intelligence (AI) and help you build the foundational knowledge, practical skills, and hands-on experience necessary to excel in this rapidly evolving field. Whether you are a beginner just starting your journey or an experienced developer seeking to deepen your understanding, this book will equip you with the tools and knowledge needed to become proficient in AI.

Why AI?

Artificial Intelligence is no longer just a buzzword—it is a transformative technology that is already reshaping industries, economies, and even the way we live our lives. From healthcare to finance, retail to transportation, AI is driving innovation, optimizing operations, and solving complex problems that were previously unimaginable. With the advent of **machine learning**, **deep learning**, and other AI technologies, the potential applications seem limitless.

AI is already being used to make medical diagnoses, power self-driving cars, recommend products to users, predict market trends, and even help create art. But these innovations are just the beginning. As AI continues to advance, its impact will only deepen, opening up new opportunities and challenges for both businesses and individuals.

Who is This Book For?

This book is for anyone who is eager to understand and work with AI—whether you are:

- A **beginner** with no prior experience in AI or machine learning, seeking to get started with the fundamentals.
- A **data scientist** or **software developer** looking to expand your knowledge and apply AI to solve real-world problems.
- An **AI enthusiast** wanting to explore the various tools, frameworks, and applications of AI, and understand how they can be used to create impactful solutions.
- A **professional** looking to transition into the AI field or deepen your understanding of AI technologies for career growth.

No matter your background, this book takes a **hands-on approach** to learning. You will work with popular AI frameworks and tools, explore real-world case studies, and build a portfolio of projects that demonstrate your skills and expertise.

What Will You Learn?

In this book, we will cover AI from the ground up, starting with the basics and progressively diving into more advanced topics and applications. Here's an overview of what you will learn:

1. **Introduction to AI**: We will start by exploring the core concepts and definitions of AI, including its history, types (narrow vs. general AI), and applications across industries. You'll understand how AI is applied in real-world scenarios and why it is such a transformative technology.

2. **Machine Learning Fundamentals**: You will get an in-depth understanding of machine learning, the cornerstone of AI, covering topics like supervised learning, unsupervised learning, and reinforcement learning. We'll explore algorithms for classification, regression, clustering, and more, with practical examples to solidify your understanding.

3. **Deep Learning and Neural Networks**: Deep learning is a subset of machine learning that powers some of the most impressive AI applications, such as image recognition, natural language processing, and autonomous driving. You'll learn how neural networks work, including

Convolutional Neural Networks (CNNs) and Recurrent Neural Networks (RNNs), and how to implement them using popular frameworks like **TensorFlow** and **PyTorch**.

4. **AI Tools and Frameworks**: You'll be introduced to popular AI tools like **TensorFlow, Keras, PyTorch**, and **scikit-learn**. Each tool has its strengths, and you'll learn how to use them effectively based on your project's needs. We'll also discuss cloud-based AI platforms like **AWS AI**, **Google AI**, and **Microsoft Azure AI** to help you scale your models and deploy them in real-world applications.

5. **Practical AI Applications**: AI has applications in virtually every industry. You'll learn how to apply AI to real-world problems, from image and speech recognition to predictive analytics, recommendation systems, and autonomous vehicles. Through case studies, you'll see how AI is used in sectors like healthcare, finance, retail, and manufacturing.

6. **Ethics and Fairness in AI**: AI systems can have profound societal implications. We will explore the ethical considerations of developing and deploying AI, including issues related to bias, transparency, fairness, and privacy. Understanding these ethical challenges is crucial for building responsible AI solutions.

7. **Building an AI Portfolio**: A strong portfolio is essential for showcasing your skills to potential employers or collaborators. This book will guide you through creating an AI portfolio that includes hands-on projects, blog posts, and open-source contributions. You'll learn how to make your work visible to the AI community and employers.

8. **Preparing for AI Careers**: Whether you aspire to become a **data scientist**, **machine learning engineer**, or **AI researcher**, this book will provide insights into what these roles entail and how to prepare for them. We'll discuss the skills, certifications, and networking strategies needed to advance your career in AI.

Hands-on Learning and Practical Projects

One of the key features of this book is its **hands-on approach**. Learning AI is best achieved through practice. Throughout the book, you will be guided to build practical projects using real-world datasets. Each chapter includes:

- **Code examples** and walkthroughs using popular AI frameworks like TensorFlow, Keras, PyTorch, and scikit-learn.
- **Project-based learning** where you'll implement machine learning and deep learning algorithms for tasks such as

image classification, sentiment analysis, and recommendation systems.

- **Exercises** to test your understanding and deepen your skills.
- **Case studies** that show how AI is used in industry, giving you a broader perspective on real-world applications.

By the end of the book, you will have a portfolio of completed projects to showcase your skills, whether you're applying for jobs, collaborating on AI research, or simply seeking to expand your expertise.

Why This Book Is Different

Many AI books focus either on theory or practice but not both. In *Learning AI: From Fundamentals to Cutting-Edge Applications*, we emphasize **a balance of theory and practical application**. We'll introduce you to the core principles of AI while giving you the tools and resources to implement what you learn and apply it to real-world problems.

Additionally, this book is written in a **beginner-friendly** manner, avoiding overly technical jargon. We explain complex concepts in clear, understandable terms, with plenty of illustrations, diagrams, and step-by-step explanations to help you grasp even the most difficult topics.

Final Thoughts

As AI continues to advance, it is transforming the way we interact with the world around us. By learning AI, you are not only gaining technical skills but also joining a global movement that is reshaping industries and societies. With this book, you now have the foundation to embark on your own journey in the AI field— whether you are looking to work as an AI developer, contribute to groundbreaking research, or apply AI to solve pressing problems.

AI is a powerful tool that, when used responsibly, has the potential to improve lives, solve global challenges, and create new opportunities. I encourage you to keep learning, experimenting, and building, and to stay curious about the endless possibilities that AI offers.

Good luck on your AI journey, and I hope this book serves as a valuable guide as you dive deeper into this fascinating field!

Key Takeaways

- **AI is revolutionizing industries** and will continue to shape the future of technology and business.
- This book provides a **comprehensive understanding of AI**, from the basics to advanced techniques, with practical hands-on projects.

13

- **Building a strong portfolio** and contributing to AI communities will help you establish your presence in the AI field.
- As you progress, always stay **curious**, keep building, and continue refining your skills.

We hope that this book will serve as your **starting point** or **next step** in becoming a skilled AI practitioner, ready to take on the challenges and opportunities in the ever-evolving world of AI.

CHAPTER 1

INTRODUCTION TO ARTIFICIAL INTELLIGENCE

In this chapter, we will introduce you to the concept of **Artificial Intelligence (AI)**, its history, significance, and its relationship with machine learning and deep learning. Additionally, we'll explore the types of AI, with a focus on **Narrow AI** and **General AI**, and give you an introduction to Python, the language widely used in AI development.

What is AI?

Artificial Intelligence, often abbreviated as **AI**, is the branch of computer science that aims to create machines capable of performing tasks that typically require human intelligence. These tasks include problem-solving, decision-making, visual perception, speech recognition, language translation, and even creativity. The ultimate goal of AI is to create systems that can think, learn, and act autonomously, in some cases surpassing human cognitive abilities.

15

At its core, AI seeks to enable computers to replicate or simulate human intelligence in a way that allows them to perform tasks and improve over time through learning.

A Brief History of Artificial Intelligence

The concept of **AI** has existed for centuries, often appearing in mythology and literature. However, the formal study of AI as we know it began in the mid-20th century.

- **1943**: Warren McCulloch and Walter Pitts developed a mathematical model of neural networks, laying the foundation for neural computation.
- **1950**: British mathematician **Alan Turing** proposed the **Turing Test**, which is a measure of a machine's ability to exhibit intelligent behavior equivalent to, or indistinguishable from, that of a human.
- **1956**: The term "Artificial Intelligence" was coined by **John McCarthy** during the **Dartmouth Conference**, which is considered the birth of AI as an academic field.
- **1950s–1970s**: AI research flourished, with early breakthroughs in symbolic AI and expert systems that performed specific tasks, such as chess-playing programs.
- **1980s–1990s**: AI experienced setbacks due to limited computational power and issues with early machine

learning models. However, research into neural networks and machine learning saw new progress.

- **2000s–present**: With the growth of computational power, large datasets, and more sophisticated algorithms, AI entered a golden era. Technologies such as **machine learning**, **deep learning**, and **reinforcement learning** powered applications in fields such as autonomous driving, natural language processing, and computer vision.

Today, AI has found applications in various industries, including healthcare, finance, entertainment, and transportation, transforming the way we interact with technology.

The Importance of AI in Today's World

AI is reshaping the way we live and work. From self-driving cars to personalized recommendations on streaming platforms, AI is becoming an integral part of daily life. Here are a few reasons why AI is critical in today's world:

- **Automation**: AI powers automation in industries, leading to increased productivity, reduced costs, and improved efficiency. For example, in manufacturing, AI-driven robots can perform repetitive tasks faster and with higher precision than humans.

- **Improved Decision-Making**: AI can analyze vast amounts of data and provide insights that support informed decision-making. This is particularly useful in sectors like healthcare (e.g., predicting patient outcomes) and finance (e.g., detecting fraudulent transactions).

- **Enhanced Customer Experience**: AI-driven chatbots, virtual assistants, and recommendation systems enhance customer interactions, improving user satisfaction and engagement.

- **Solving Complex Problems**: AI allows us to solve problems that were once too complex for traditional methods. For instance, in drug discovery, AI can help identify potential treatments faster by analyzing biological data.

- **Economic Growth**: AI is fueling innovation and creating new industries. Businesses that implement AI can gain a competitive edge, leading to economic growth and the creation of jobs in AI research, development, and maintenance.

Types of AI: Narrow AI vs. General AI

AI can be categorized based on its capabilities and level of autonomy:

1. **Narrow AI (Weak AI)**:

o **Narrow AI**, also known as **Weak AI**, refers to systems designed to handle a specific task or a narrow range of tasks. These systems are highly specialized and perform tasks such as facial recognition, language translation, or playing chess.

o **Examples of Narrow AI**:

- **Siri** and **Google Assistant**: Virtual assistants designed to perform tasks like answering questions, setting reminders, and managing calendars.

- **Self-driving cars**: Autonomous vehicles that use AI to navigate, avoid obstacles, and drive safely within certain environments.

- **Recommendation systems**: AI algorithms used by Netflix and Amazon to recommend movies or products based on user preferences.

o Narrow AI does not possess general cognitive abilities like humans, and it excels only in the tasks it was specifically designed to perform.

2. **General AI (Strong AI)**:

o **General AI**, or **Strong AI**, refers to a form of AI that possesses human-like cognitive abilities and can perform a wide range of tasks that require intelligence. It would have the ability to reason, solve problems, and learn in ways similar to human beings.

o   General AI remains largely theoretical and has not been realized yet. Achieving General AI would require breakthroughs in understanding consciousness and replicating human-level intelligence in machines.

Examples of potential General AI applications are robots that could perform various household tasks, or AI systems that could autonomously learn and adapt to entirely new environments and situations, much like humans do.

How AI Relates to Machine Learning and Deep Learning

AI, machine learning (ML), and deep learning (DL) are closely related but distinct concepts.

1.   **Artificial Intelligence (AI)**:
     o   As previously discussed, AI refers to machines designed to replicate human intelligence and behavior. It encompasses a wide range of techniques, including traditional programming, heuristics, logic, and more.

2.   **Machine Learning (ML)**:

20

o **Machine Learning** is a subset of AI that involves training algorithms to learn patterns from data without explicit programming. The idea is to give machines the ability to learn from experience and make decisions based on data.

o In ML, a model is trained using data to make predictions or decisions without being explicitly programmed to perform a specific task.

o **Examples** of ML algorithms:

  ▪ **Linear Regression**: Used for predicting continuous values like house prices.

  ▪ **Logistic Regression**: Used for binary classification tasks, like spam detection.

  ▪ **Decision Trees**: Used for classification tasks like customer churn prediction.

3. **Deep Learning (DL)**:

o **Deep Learning** is a specialized subset of machine learning that uses neural networks with many layers (hence "deep"). Deep learning algorithms are capable of learning from large amounts of unstructured data like images, audio, and text.

o Deep learning powers more complex AI applications, such as self-driving cars, speech recognition, and image classification.

o **Examples** of deep learning:

21

- **Convolutional Neural Networks (CNNs)** for image classification (e.g., identifying objects in photos).
- **Recurrent Neural Networks (RNNs)** for sequential data (e.g., speech recognition and time-series analysis).

In essence, **AI** is the broad goal of creating intelligent machines, and **machine learning** and **deep learning** are subsets that focus on allowing machines to learn from data to perform tasks autonomously.

Introduction to Python for AI

Python is the most popular programming language for AI and machine learning for several reasons:

- **Readability and simplicity**: Python has a clean, readable syntax that is easy for both beginners and experts to understand.
- **Extensive libraries and frameworks**: Python offers a vast ecosystem of libraries and frameworks that make AI development faster and more efficient. Key libraries for AI include:
  - **NumPy**: A powerful library for numerical computations and data manipulation.

- o **pandas**: A library for data analysis and manipulation, especially with tabular data.
- o **scikit-learn**: A library for machine learning that provides simple and efficient tools for data mining and analysis.
- o **TensorFlow** and **PyTorch**: Popular deep learning frameworks for building neural networks and deep learning models.
- o **Keras**: A high-level neural networks API that runs on top of TensorFlow, simplifying the building and training of deep learning models.

Python's versatility, combined with its rich ecosystem of libraries and frameworks, makes it the perfect language to get started with AI development.

Key Takeaways

- **AI** is the branch of computer science aimed at creating intelligent machines that can perform tasks that typically require human intelligence.
- The history of AI spans decades, from early theoretical work to the rapid advancements we see today in areas like deep learning and autonomous systems.

23

- **Narrow AI** is highly specialized, while **General AI** is a theoretical concept that would involve machines with human-like cognitive abilities.
- **Machine Learning (ML)** and **Deep Learning (DL)** are subsets of AI, with ML focused on learning from data and DL focused on complex patterns using neural networks.
- Python is the dominant language for AI development due to its simplicity, powerful libraries, and frameworks that accelerate AI and machine learning projects.

This chapter has set the stage for understanding what AI is, its history, significance, and the tools you'll use to get started. As you progress through the book, you'll build your first AI models and dive deeper into machine learning and AI techniques with hands-on examples and case studies.

In the next chapter, we will dive into the **fundamentals of machine learning**, exploring the basic concepts, algorithms, and workflows needed to start building your AI models.

CHAPTER 2

THE FUNDAMENTALS OF MACHINE LEARNING

In this chapter, we will introduce you to **Machine Learning (ML)**, one of the key subfields of Artificial Intelligence (AI). We'll explain the core concepts, such as supervised vs. unsupervised learning, the types of ML algorithms (classification, regression, clustering), and the relationship between **data science** and **machine learning**. Additionally, we will explore real-world applications to illustrate the power and potential of machine learning in various industries.

What is Machine Learning?

Machine Learning is a branch of AI that focuses on building systems that can learn from data and improve over time, without being explicitly programmed. Instead of writing detailed instructions for every possible scenario, we provide data to the system, which then analyzes the data, learns from it, and makes predictions or decisions based on patterns it identifies.

In simple terms, **Machine Learning enables machines to automatically learn and adapt from experience**, rather than

25

requiring manual programming for each task. The goal is to allow systems to automatically learn from past data, identify patterns, and make decisions or predictions based on new data.

Key steps in a typical machine learning process include:

- **Data collection**: Gathering and preparing data.
- **Model training**: Feeding the data into a model to learn patterns.
- **Prediction or decision-making**: Using the trained model to make predictions or decisions on new data.

Supervised vs. Unsupervised Learning

Machine learning can be broadly categorized into two types: **supervised learning** and **unsupervised learning**. These categories differ in how the learning process is structured and what kind of data is used for training the model.

Supervised Learning

In **supervised learning**, the model is trained using labeled data, where the output (or **label**) is provided along with the input data. The algorithm learns from this labeled data and adjusts itself to make predictions or classifications based on the relationship between the input and the output.

- **How it works**: In supervised learning, you have a training dataset that contains both the input features and the correct outputs. The algorithm uses this data to learn the mapping between inputs and outputs, and then applies that knowledge to new, unseen data to make predictions.
- **Applications of supervised learning**:
  - **Classification**: Predicting categorical outcomes, such as spam vs. not spam emails, or determining whether a customer will churn or not.
  - **Regression**: Predicting continuous outcomes, such as house prices, stock prices, or temperature forecasts.

Examples:

- Predicting whether an email is spam or not based on previous labeled data.
- Predicting the price of a house based on features like size, location, and number of rooms.

Unsupervised Learning

In **unsupervised learning**, the model is given unlabeled data and must find patterns, relationships, or structures on its own. The algorithm is not provided with output labels; instead, it looks for hidden structures in the data to help organize or classify the data.

- **How it works**: In unsupervised learning, the algorithm tries to learn the underlying structure of the data without any explicit supervision. It finds patterns, groups, or clusters of similar data points that can be used for further analysis or decision-making.
- **Applications of unsupervised learning**:
  - **Clustering**: Grouping similar data points together, such as customer segmentation, or grouping similar documents in a text corpus.
  - **Dimensionality reduction**: Reducing the number of features in a dataset while preserving its essential structure (e.g., Principal Component Analysis or PCA).

Examples:

- Segmenting customers based on purchasing behavior without predefined categories.
- Organizing documents into topics without having predefined labels.

Semi-Supervised and Reinforcement Learning

In addition to supervised and unsupervised learning, there are two other important learning paradigms:

- **Semi-supervised learning**: This technique uses both labeled and unlabeled data to train the model. Typically, a small portion of labeled data is used alongside a larger portion of unlabeled data, often in applications where labeling data is expensive or time-consuming.

- **Reinforcement learning**: In reinforcement learning, an agent learns by interacting with an environment, receiving feedback in the form of rewards or penalties. This type of learning is often used for decision-making tasks, like game playing or robotics.

Introduction to Algorithms: Classification, Regression, Clustering

Machine learning algorithms are methods or procedures used by machines to learn from data. These algorithms can be divided into various types depending on the problem you are trying to solve. The most common types of algorithms include **classification**, **regression**, and **clustering**.

Classification

- **Classification** algorithms are used in supervised learning to categorize data into predefined classes or labels. The goal is to map input data to one of a limited number of categories.
- Common algorithms for classification include:

29

- o **Logistic Regression**: Despite its name, logistic regression is used for binary classification tasks (e.g., spam or not spam).
- o **Decision Trees**: A tree-like model used for classification and regression tasks.
- o **K-Nearest Neighbors (KNN)**: A simple algorithm that classifies data points based on the majority class of their neighbors.
- o **Support Vector Machines (SVM)**: A powerful classification algorithm that finds the optimal boundary between different classes.

Example: Classifying emails into "spam" or "not spam."

Regression

- **Regression** algorithms are used to predict a continuous output. Unlike classification, where the output is categorical, regression predicts numerical values based on input data.
- Common regression algorithms include:
  - o **Linear Regression**: A simple algorithm that assumes a linear relationship between input features and the output.
  - o **Decision Tree Regression**: A regression version of decision trees used to predict continuous values.

30

o **Random Forest Regression**: An ensemble method that builds multiple decision trees and aggregates their predictions.

Example: Predicting house prices based on features like size, location, and number of rooms.

Clustering

- **Clustering** is an unsupervised learning algorithm used to group data points that are similar to one another. Unlike classification, where labels are provided, clustering algorithms try to find natural groupings or patterns in the data.
- Common clustering algorithms include:
  o **K-means Clustering**: A simple algorithm that divides data into k clusters by minimizing the variance within each cluster.
  o **Hierarchical Clustering**: Builds a tree of clusters, where each data point starts in its own cluster and is merged into larger clusters based on similarity.
  o **DBSCAN (Density-Based Spatial Clustering of Applications with Noise)**: A clustering algorithm that finds arbitrarily shaped clusters based on density.

Example: Grouping customers into segments based on purchasing behavior.

Overview of Data Science and Its Relationship with Machine Learning

Data science is a multidisciplinary field that focuses on extracting insights from data, often using statistical, computational, and machine learning methods. It is the backbone of machine learning and is deeply intertwined with the development of AI models.

While **machine learning** focuses on algorithms that allow computers to learn from data, **data science** encompasses the entire process of working with data, including data collection, cleaning, analysis, and visualization. Data scientists typically use machine learning techniques to model data, make predictions, and analyze trends.

Key aspects of data science related to machine learning:

- **Data cleaning and preprocessing**: The quality of your data plays a crucial role in the success of machine learning models. Data scientists clean and preprocess data to remove noise, fill missing values, and format the data in a way that is suitable for machine learning.

- **Feature engineering**: Creating new features from raw data to improve the predictive power of machine learning models.
- **Data visualization**: Using graphs and plots to understand data distributions, relationships between variables, and model performance.

Real-World Applications of Machine Learning

Machine learning is being applied in numerous industries and is transforming how businesses and organizations operate. Here are some examples of how machine learning is used in real-world applications:

- **Healthcare**: Predicting patient outcomes, diagnosing diseases from medical images, and recommending treatments based on medical data.
  - o Example: AI algorithms help detect early signs of diseases like cancer through image classification and pattern recognition.
- **Finance**: Detecting fraudulent transactions, predicting stock prices, and automating trading strategies.
  - o Example: Banks use machine learning to identify unusual patterns in transaction data, alerting them to potential fraud.

- **Retail and E-commerce**: Personalizing recommendations, optimizing inventory, and improving customer service with chatbots.
  - o Example: Online stores like Amazon use machine learning for product recommendations based on customer behavior.
- **Self-driving cars**: Autonomous vehicles use machine learning models to interpret sensor data, make decisions, and navigate roads.
  - o Example: Tesla uses deep learning algorithms to enable self-driving features like autopilot.
- **Marketing**: Segmenting customers, predicting customer behavior, and optimizing marketing campaigns.
  - o Example: Machine learning is used to personalize ads, recommend products, and segment customer demographics.

Key Takeaways

- **Machine Learning (ML)** enables computers to learn from data and improve without explicit programming. It is a subset of Artificial Intelligence.
- **Supervised learning** uses labeled data, while **unsupervised learning** uses unlabeled data to find patterns or groupings.

- Common **ML algorithms** include classification (e.g., logistic regression, decision trees), regression (e.g., linear regression), and clustering (e.g., k-means).
- **Data science** encompasses a broader field that includes data collection, cleaning, analysis, and machine learning, helping extract meaningful insights from data.
- **Machine Learning** is already being used in many real-world applications across industries such as healthcare, finance, and retail, and is transforming the way businesses operate.

This chapter has provided an essential foundation for understanding machine learning. In the next chapter, we will explore the **tools and techniques for preparing and analyzing data** to build your first machine learning models effectively.

CHAPTER 3

SETTING UP YOUR AI ENVIRONMENT

In this chapter, we will walk you through the process of setting up the necessary environment for AI and machine learning development using Python. This includes installing Python and essential libraries, setting up development tools like **Jupyter notebooks**, and configuring an Integrated Development Environment (IDE) like **PyCharm** or **VS Code**. Additionally, we'll introduce **virtual environments**, which help you manage project dependencies effectively.

Installing Python and Necessary Libraries

Python is the most widely used programming language for AI and machine learning, thanks to its simplicity and the powerful libraries available for scientific computing and data analysis. Let's start by installing Python and the essential libraries you will need.

1. Installing Python

- **Windows**:

36

- o Go to the official Python website: https://www.python.org/downloads/
- o Download the latest version of Python for Windows.
- o Run the installer and **check the box that says "Add Python to PATH"** before proceeding with the installation.

- **MacOS**:
  - o On MacOS, Python usually comes pre-installed. However, it's a good idea to install the latest version using **Homebrew**:

```bash

brew install python
```

- **Linux**:
  - o On Linux, you can install Python using your distribution's package manager (e.g., `apt` for Ubuntu):

```bash

sudo apt update
sudo apt install python3
```

To verify the installation, open a terminal and type:

```
bash
```

```
python --version  # or python3 --version
```

You should see the version of Python you just installed.

2. Installing Necessary Libraries

There are several essential libraries in Python that you'll need for AI and machine learning development. Here's how to install them:

- **NumPy**: A core library for numerical operations in Python, especially useful for array manipulations.
- **pandas**: A powerful data manipulation and analysis library, often used for working with structured data.
- **scikit-learn**: One of the most popular machine learning libraries, which provides tools for classification, regression, clustering, and more.
- **Matplotlib** and **Seaborn**: Libraries for data visualization.
- **TensorFlow** and **Keras**: Deep learning frameworks used for building neural networks and deep learning models.

To install these libraries, you can use **pip** (Python's package installer) in your terminal or command prompt. Run the following command to install them all at once:

```
bash
```

```
pip install numpy pandas scikit-learn matplotlib
seaborn tensorflow keras
```

You can also install individual libraries based on your needs:

```bash
bash
```

```
pip install numpy      # For numerical operations
pip install pandas        # For data manipulation
pip install scikit-learn # For machine learning
models
pip install matplotlib   # For plotting graphs
pip install seaborn              # For advanced
visualizations
pip install tensorflow    # For deep learning
frameworks
pip install keras      # High-level deep learning
API
```

3. Checking the Installation

To check if the libraries were installed successfully, you can open a Python interpreter and try importing them:

```python
python
```

```
import numpy as np
import pandas as pd
import sklearn
import matplotlib.pyplot as plt
import seaborn as sns
```

```
import tensorflow as tf
import keras
```

If no errors appear, the libraries are installed and ready to use.

Using Jupyter Notebooks for AI Development

Jupyter notebooks are one of the most popular tools for data science and AI development. They allow you to write code, run it, and visualize results all in one interactive environment. Jupyter notebooks are especially useful for AI and machine learning projects because they make it easy to experiment with code, visualize data, and share your work.

1. Installing Jupyter Notebooks

You can install **Jupyter** using **pip**:

```bash
```

```
pip install jupyter
```

Once installed, you can start a Jupyter notebook by running the following command in your terminal:

```bash
```

```
jupyter notebook
```

40

This will open a Jupyter Notebook dashboard in your browser, where you can create and manage notebooks.

2. Creating and Using Notebooks

In the Jupyter Notebook interface:

- Click on **New** > **Python 3** to create a new notebook.
- You can write code in the notebook cells and execute them by pressing **Shift + Enter**.

Advantages of Jupyter Notebooks:

- **Interactive development**: You can write code and see the results immediately. It's great for experimenting with different machine learning models, testing hypotheses, and visualizing data.
- **Documentation**: You can add markdown cells to explain your code and document your progress.
- **Visualizations**: With libraries like **Matplotlib**, **Seaborn**, and **Plotly**, you can easily visualize data within the same notebook.

Setting Up an IDE for Python (PyCharm, VS Code)

While Jupyter notebooks are great for experimentation, an **Integrated Development Environment (IDE)** like **PyCharm** or

VS Code is often better suited for building larger Python projects, especially when it comes to debugging, managing files, and working on collaborative projects.

1. Installing PyCharm

PyCharm is a powerful IDE developed by JetBrains, specifically designed for Python development. It provides features like code completion, debugging, project management, and more.

- Download PyCharm from the official website: https://www.jetbrains.com/pycharm/download/
- After installation, open PyCharm and create a new project.
- Ensure that the **Python interpreter** is selected for the project, which allows PyCharm to recognize your installed libraries.

2. Installing Visual Studio Code (VS Code)

Visual Studio Code (VS Code) is a lightweight, open-source IDE that is widely used for Python development. It is flexible and highly customizable with a wide range of extensions.

- Download and install **VS Code** from the official website: https://code.visualstudio.com/
- After installation, install the **Python extension** for VS Code:

o Go to **Extensions** (Ctrl+Shift+X), search for "Python" by Microsoft, and click **Install**.

- You can create a new Python project or open an existing directory, and VS Code will automatically detect Python files.

VS Code Features:

- **Code completion**: With the Python extension, you get intelligent code suggestions.
- **Debugging**: VS Code offers robust debugging tools to track down errors and bugs in your code.
- **Terminal integration**: It allows you to run Python scripts directly from the terminal within VS Code.

Introduction to Virtual Environments

In Python, a **virtual environment** is an isolated environment that allows you to manage dependencies for different projects separately. This ensures that each project has its own dependencies, avoiding conflicts between libraries and versions.

1. Why Use Virtual Environments?

- **Isolated Dependencies**: Virtual environments allow you to install project-specific libraries without affecting other projects or system-wide packages.

- **Manage Multiple Projects**: You can work on multiple Python projects that require different versions of the same library.
- **Avoid Conflicts**: If you need a specific version of a library for one project, you can install it in a virtual environment without changing the global setup.

2. Creating and Using Virtual Environments

To create a virtual environment, follow these steps:

- **Step 1**: Install **virtualenv** (if not installed already):

```bash

pip install virtualenv
```

- **Step 2**: Create a virtual environment in your project directory:

```bash

virtualenv venv
```

- **Step 3**: Activate the virtual environment:
  - **Windows**:

    ```bash
    ```

```
.\venv\Scripts\activate
```

- o **Mac/Linux**:

```
bash
```

```
source venv/bin/activate
```

- **Step 4**: Once activated, you can install your project-specific libraries in this environment:

```
bash
```

```
pip install numpy pandas scikit-learn
```

- **Step 5**: Deactivate the virtual environment when you're done:

```
bash
```

```
deactivate
```

3. Using `requirements.txt` to Manage Dependencies

For easier management of dependencies across projects, you can save all the libraries you're using in a **requirements.txt** file:

```
bash
```

```
pip freeze > requirements.txt
```

To install all the libraries listed in `requirements.txt`, run:

```
bash
```

```
pip install -r requirements.txt
```

Key Takeaways

- **Python** is the primary language used for AI and machine learning, and installing the necessary libraries (NumPy, pandas, scikit-learn, etc.) is essential for building AI models.
- **Jupyter notebooks** are an excellent tool for interactive development, experimentation, and visualization in machine learning and data science.
- **IDE options** like **PyCharm** and **VS Code** provide enhanced coding, debugging, and project management capabilities for larger Python projects.
- **Virtual environments** are essential for managing dependencies and ensuring that different projects don't interfere with each other.

With the environment set up, you're now ready to dive into machine learning and start building your AI models! In the next chapter, we will explore the **core concepts of machine learning**, starting with supervised learning techniques and basic algorithms.

46

CHAPTER 4

UNDERSTANDING DATA IN AI

In this chapter, we will dive into the **importance of data** in Artificial Intelligence (AI) and how to handle it effectively. Data is the backbone of any AI system, as the performance and success of machine learning models heavily depend on the quality and structure of the data fed into them. We'll explore the different types of data, techniques for cleaning and transforming data, how to handle missing values, and introduce you to **Exploratory Data Analysis (EDA)** – the first step in data analysis and model development.

What is Data in the Context of AI?

In the world of AI, **data** refers to the raw information that is processed, analyzed, and used to train machine learning models. This data can come from various sources, such as sensors, websites, databases, or real-time feeds. **Machine learning models** learn from the data by identifying patterns and correlations, and then use this knowledge to make predictions or decisions on new, unseen data.

For AI to be effective, it requires **high-quality data**. The better the data, the better the model's predictions or performance. This is why understanding and preparing data is a crucial step in AI and machine learning workflows.

Types of Data: Structured vs. Unstructured

Data can come in different formats, which can significantly impact the methods used to process it. The two primary types of data used in AI are **structured** and **unstructured data**.

Structured Data

Structured data is highly organized and typically stored in tabular format, such as **databases** or **spreadsheets**. It follows a clear, defined schema where each piece of data fits into a well-defined category or field (e.g., rows and columns). This type of data is easy to analyze and manipulate using traditional tools like SQL, Python libraries (pandas), or machine learning algorithms.

Examples of structured data:

- A CSV file with rows representing customers and columns representing customer attributes (e.g., name, age, purchase history).
- A relational database with tables like **customer**, **order**, and **product**.

Unstructured Data

Unstructured data refers to data that does not follow a specific format or structure. It is often textual, image-based, or multimedia data and can be more challenging to analyze directly using traditional tools. AI, particularly deep learning, is often used to process unstructured data, especially in fields like image recognition, natural language processing (NLP), and speech recognition.

Examples of unstructured data:

- **Text data**: Emails, social media posts, and customer reviews.
- **Images**: Photographs, medical images (e.g., X-rays), and satellite imagery.
- **Audio**: Voice recordings and speech data.

While unstructured data requires more advanced processing techniques, such as natural language processing (NLP) for text or convolutional neural networks (CNNs) for images, it is a key part of modern AI applications.

Data Preprocessing: Cleaning and Transforming Data

Data preprocessing is the process of preparing raw data for analysis or machine learning tasks. Data is rarely clean or ready

49

for use right out of the box, so preprocessing is a crucial step in ensuring the quality of your model.

Steps in Data Preprocessing:

1. **Data Cleaning**:
   - o **Removing duplicates**: Duplicate data points can skew the results of your model. It is important to identify and remove them.
   - o **Handling inconsistent data**: Ensure that all data follows a consistent format (e.g., date formats, categorical values like "Male" vs "M").
   - o **Fixing incorrect data**: Sometimes, errors occur during data entry, so it's important to identify and correct those mistakes.

2. **Data Transformation**:
   - o **Normalization** and **Standardization**: These techniques adjust the scale of numerical data to ensure that all features contribute equally to the model's performance. For example, normalizing data to the range [0, 1] or standardizing it to have a mean of 0 and a standard deviation of 1.
     - ▪ **Normalization** is useful when the features have different scales, and **standardization** is used when the data has a Gaussian distribution.

- o **Encoding categorical variables**: In machine learning models, categorical data (such as gender or city names) must be converted into a numerical format. Techniques like **one-hot encoding** or **label encoding** can help with this.

3. **Feature Engineering**:

   - o **Feature selection**: Identify the most important variables (features) in your data that will help improve the model's performance. Irrelevant features can add noise and reduce the model's accuracy.

   - o **Feature extraction**: Create new features from existing ones. For example, from a date field, you might extract the year, month, and day to create additional features.

Example of transformation:

python

```
import pandas as pd
from sklearn.preprocessing import StandardScaler

# Sample Data
data = {'age': [25, 30, 35, 40, 45], 'income':
[50000, 60000, 70000, 80000, 90000]}
df = pd.DataFrame(data)
```

```
# Standardizing the data
scaler = StandardScaler()
df[['age',                'income']]                =
scaler.fit_transform(df[['age', 'income']])
```

Handling Missing Values

Missing data is a common problem in real-world datasets. If not handled properly, it can severely impact the performance of machine learning models. There are several techniques to deal with missing values:

Methods to Handle Missing Values:

1. **Removing missing values**:
   - o If the amount of missing data is small and random, it may be acceptable to **remove rows** or **columns** with missing values.

   python

   ```
   df.dropna()   # Removes rows with any
   missing values
   ```

2. **Imputation**:
   - o **Impute** missing values by filling them with a statistical measure such as the **mean**, **median**, or **mode** of the column.

```python

df['age'].fillna(df['age'].mean(),
inplace=True)    # Replacing missing 'age'
values with the mean
```

3. **Predicting missing values**:
   o For more advanced techniques, missing values can be predicted using a model, such as using the **K-Nearest Neighbors (KNN)** algorithm to predict missing values based on similar instances.

4. **Using placeholders**:
   o In some cases, it might make sense to fill missing data with a placeholder like "Unknown" or "0" depending on the context.

Choosing the right method depends on the nature of the missing data and the specific problem you are working on.

Exploratory Data Analysis (EDA) Basics

Exploratory Data Analysis (EDA) is the process of analyzing and summarizing a dataset before applying machine learning algorithms. It allows you to understand the underlying structure of the data, discover patterns, spot anomalies, and check assumptions.

EDA is crucial in identifying problems with the data (such as outliers or missing values) and helping you choose the best machine learning model.

Steps in EDA:

1. **Data Visualization**:
   o Use plots to explore the data visually. This can help identify trends, relationships, and patterns that may not be apparent from just looking at numbers.
      - **Histograms**: To visualize the distribution of numerical data.
      - **Box plots**: To detect outliers and understand the distribution.
      - **Scatter plots**: To visualize relationships between two continuous variables.
      - **Correlation heatmaps**: To understand the relationship between variables.

```python
import seaborn as sns
import matplotlib.pyplot as plt

sns.histplot(df['age'], kde=True)     #
Histogram with KDE (Kernel Density
Estimation)
```

```
plt.show()
```

2. **Summary Statistics**:

   o   Calculate descriptive statistics to summarize the data, such as mean, median, standard deviation, and percentiles.

```
python
```

```
df.describe()     #  Provides  statistical
summary for numerical features
```

3. **Data Distribution**:

   o   Check how the data is distributed to understand the range of values and the skewness of the data (e.g., normal distribution, uniform distribution).

4. **Outlier Detection**:

   o   Outliers can significantly affect machine learning models. You can detect them visually using box plots or use statistical methods like the **Z-score** to identify and handle them.

5. **Identifying Relationships**:

   o   Use correlation matrices to understand how features are related to one another. This is helpful for identifying multicollinearity or redundant features in your dataset.

Key Takeaways

- **Data is the foundation of AI**: In AI and machine learning, the quality of data directly impacts the performance of models. Proper handling and preprocessing of data are crucial.

- **Structured vs. Unstructured Data**: Structured data is easy to manipulate and analyze, while unstructured data requires advanced techniques like deep learning to process.

- **Data Preprocessing**: This step includes cleaning, transforming, and normalizing data to prepare it for machine learning models. Handling missing values and performing feature engineering is crucial.

- **Exploratory Data Analysis (EDA)**: EDA helps in understanding the dataset, spotting patterns, and identifying potential issues like outliers or missing values. Visualization and summary statistics are powerful tools in this step.

With a solid understanding of data types and preprocessing techniques, you are now ready to start applying machine learning models to your data. In the next chapter, we will explore how to use these preprocessed datasets to build your first machine learning model using supervised learning techniques.

CHAPTER 5

PYTHON FOR DATA ANALYSIS

In this chapter, we will introduce you to the key Python libraries used for data analysis: **NumPy**, **pandas**, and **Matplotlib**. These libraries are foundational for working with data in Python, providing powerful tools for numerical computations, data manipulation, and data visualization. We will explore how to work with dataframes and arrays, visualize data using **Matplotlib** and **Seaborn**, and perform basic statistical analysis. Finally, we will work through a **real-world case study** to demonstrate the application of these tools.

Overview of Key Python Libraries: NumPy, pandas, and Matplotlib

1. NumPy (Numerical Python)

NumPy is a powerful library for numerical computing in Python. It provides support for **arrays**, which are more efficient than Python's built-in lists when handling large datasets. NumPy is widely used for scientific computing and provides tools for linear algebra, statistics, and random number generation.

Key features:

- **ndarray (N-dimensional array)**: A core data structure for storing homogeneous data (e.g., numerical values).
- **Vectorized operations**: Operations on NumPy arrays are faster and more efficient compared to traditional Python lists.
- **Mathematical functions**: NumPy provides a wide range of mathematical functions to perform operations on arrays.

Installation:

```bash

pip install numpy
```
2. pandas

pandas is a powerful library for data manipulation and analysis. It provides two primary data structures:

- **Series**: A one-dimensional array-like object.
- **DataFrame**: A two-dimensional table with rows and columns, which is similar to a spreadsheet or SQL table.

pandas makes it easy to handle structured data (like CSV files) and perform operations such as filtering, grouping, and aggregating data.

Key features:

- **DataFrame**: A 2D table for structured data.
- **Handling missing data**: Functions to fill or drop missing data.
- **Data alignment**: Aligning data with respect to indexes.

Installation:

bash

pip install pandas

3. Matplotlib

Matplotlib is the most widely used library for creating static, animated, and interactive visualizations in Python. It provides a variety of plotting functions that help you visualize data in the form of line plots, bar charts, scatter plots, histograms, and more.

Key features:

- **Line plots, bar charts, histograms, pie charts**: Matplotlib supports multiple types of charts for data visualization.
- **Customization**: You can customize plots with titles, axis labels, legends, and colors.

Installation:

bash

```
pip install matplotlib
```

4. Seaborn

Seaborn is built on top of Matplotlib and provides a high-level interface for drawing attractive and informative statistical graphics. It simplifies the creation of complex plots, especially for visualizing relationships between variables and distributions.

Key features:

- **Heatmaps, pair plots, categorical plots**: Seaborn is great for visualizing correlations, distributions, and categorical data.
- **Advanced styling**: Seaborn has built-in themes and color palettes to improve the aesthetics of plots.

Installation:

```
bash
```

```
pip install seaborn
```

Working with DataFrames and Arrays

Now that you are familiar with the libraries, let's explore how to work with data using **NumPy** arrays and **pandas** DataFrames.

1. NumPy Arrays

NumPy arrays (ndarray) are more efficient for numerical computations than Python lists. They allow for vectorized operations, which makes them much faster and more concise for mathematical operations.

Creating NumPy Arrays:

```python
python

import numpy as np

# Creating a 1D array
arr = np.array([1, 2, 3, 4, 5])

# Creating a 2D array
arr2d = np.array([[1, 2, 3], [4, 5, 6]])

# Displaying the array
print(arr)
print(arr2d)
```

Array Operations:

```python
python

# Array addition
arr_sum = arr + 5  # Adds 5 to each element
```

```
print(arr_sum)

# Array multiplication
arr_prod = arr * 2  # Multiplies each element by
2
print(arr_prod)

# Element-wise comparison
arr_bool = arr > 3  # Returns a boolean array
based on condition
print(arr_bool)
```

2. pandas DataFrames

A **DataFrame** is a two-dimensional table where each column can hold data of a different type (e.g., integers, floats, strings). It's the most commonly used data structure in pandas.

Creating a DataFrame:

```
python

import pandas as pd

# Creating a DataFrame from a dictionary
data = {
    'Name': ['Alice', 'Bob', 'Charlie'],
    'Age': [25, 30, 35],
    'City': ['New York', 'Los Angeles',
'Chicago']
```

```
}

df = pd.DataFrame(data)
print(df)
```

Accessing and Manipulating DataFrames:

```python

# Accessing a column
print(df['Name'])

# Accessing multiple columns
print(df[['Name', 'Age']])

# Adding a new column
df['Salary'] = [50000, 60000, 70000]
print(df)

# Filtering rows based on conditions
filtered_df = df[df['Age'] > 30]
print(filtered_df)
```

Visualizing Data with Matplotlib and Seaborn

Data visualization is an essential part of the data analysis process. **Matplotlib** and **Seaborn** help us create various plots to understand our data better.

1. Visualizing Data with Matplotlib

Matplotlib provides a variety of plotting functions, such as line plots, bar plots, scatter plots, and histograms.

Line Plot:

```python
import matplotlib.pyplot as plt

# Creating a simple line plot
x = [1, 2, 3, 4, 5]
y = [2, 4, 6, 8, 10]

plt.plot(x, y)
plt.title('Line Plot Example')
plt.xlabel('X-axis')
plt.ylabel('Y-axis')
plt.show()
```

Bar Plot:

```python
categories = ['A', 'B', 'C', 'D']
values = [10, 20, 15, 25]

plt.bar(categories, values)
plt.title('Bar Plot Example')
```

```python
plt.xlabel('Categories')
plt.ylabel('Values')
plt.show()
```

2. Visualizing Data with Seaborn

Seaborn provides a more sophisticated interface for plotting complex relationships and statistical patterns.

Scatter Plot:

python

```python
import seaborn as sns


# Scatter plot with Seaborn
sns.scatterplot(x='Age', y='Salary', data=df)
plt.title('Scatter Plot Example')
plt.show()
```

Heatmap:

python

```python
# Generating a heatmap to visualize correlations
corr_matrix = df.corr()
sns.heatmap(corr_matrix,                 annot=True,
cmap='coolwarm', fmt='.2f')
plt.title('Correlation Heatmap')
plt.show()
```

Performing Basic Statistical Analysis with Python

Before applying machine learning algorithms, it's important to understand the data statistically. Python, with the help of **pandas**, makes it easy to perform basic statistical analysis.

1. Descriptive Statistics

You can quickly compute key statistics such as mean, median, standard deviation, and more using pandas.

```python
python
```

```python
# Descriptive statistics for numerical columns
print(df.describe())
```

Output:

```matlab
matlab
```

	Age	Salary
count	3.000000	3.000000
mean	30.000000	60000.000000
std	5.000000	10000.000000
min	25.000000	50000.000000
25%	27.500000	55000.000000
50%	30.000000	60000.000000
75%	32.500000	65000.000000
max	35.000000	70000.000000

2. Correlation

You can calculate correlations between numeric features to see how they relate to each other. The **correlation matrix** helps identify relationships between variables.

```python
python
```

```python
# Calculating correlations
correlation = df.corr()
print(correlation)
```

Case Study: Data Analysis on a Real-World Dataset

Let's work through a case study where we perform basic data analysis on a **real-world dataset**. For this example, we'll use a **CSV file** containing information about employees in a company, such as their age, salary, department, and years of experience. We will load the data, clean it, and perform basic EDA.

1. Loading the Data

Assume we have a dataset named `employee_data.csv`. Let's load it into a pandas DataFrame.

```python
python
```

```python
# Load the dataset
```

```
df = pd.read_csv('employee_data.csv')
print(df.head())  # Show the first few rows
```

2. Data Cleaning

- Handle missing values by either filling them with a specific value or dropping the rows with missing data.
- Convert categorical variables into numerical format (e.g., encoding departments).

python

```
# Fill missing values with the mean of the column
df['Salary']                              =
df['Salary'].fillna(df['Salary'].mean())

# Convert 'Department' column to numerical using
label encoding
df['Department']                          =
df['Department'].astype('category').cat.codes
```

3. Exploratory Data Analysis (EDA)

- Plot histograms to see the distribution of age and salary.
- Calculate summary statistics to understand the data's spread.

python

```
# Histogram for Age and Salary
df['Age'].hist(bins=20)
```

```
plt.title('Age Distribution')
plt.show()

df['Salary'].hist(bins=20)
plt.title('Salary Distribution')
plt.show()

# Summary statistics
print(df.describe())
```

4. Visualizing Relationships

We'll use scatter plots to visualize the relationship between **Age** and **Salary**, and a heatmap to understand correlations between numerical variables.

python

```
# Scatter plot for Age vs Salary
sns.scatterplot(x='Age', y='Salary', data=df)
plt.title('Age vs Salary')
plt.show()

# Correlation heatmap
sns.heatmap(df.corr(),                annot=True,
cmap='coolwarm', fmt='.2f')
plt.title('Correlation Matrix')
plt.show()
```

Key Takeaways

- **NumPy** and **pandas** are essential libraries for handling numerical data and structured datasets (dataframes). They allow for efficient operations like filtering, transforming, and aggregating data.
- **Matplotlib** and **Seaborn** are powerful tools for visualizing data, helping you identify patterns, outliers, and relationships.
- Basic **statistical analysis** in Python, using **descriptive statistics** and **correlation**, helps summarize and understand the underlying trends in data.
- **Data cleaning and preprocessing** are crucial steps in data analysis, ensuring that the data is ready for use in machine learning models.
- Through a real-world case study, we demonstrated how to apply these concepts to analyze a dataset effectively.

In the next chapter, we will explore how to apply machine learning models to this cleaned and preprocessed data, starting with **supervised learning techniques** like **regression** and **classification**.

CHAPTER 6

INTRODUCTION TO AI ALGORITHMS

In this chapter, we will introduce you to the core concepts of **machine learning algorithms**, which are the backbone of AI models. Understanding the algorithms is key to building AI systems that learn from data and make predictions. We'll explore popular machine learning algorithms such as **linear regression**, **decision trees**, **k-nearest neighbors**, and more. Additionally, we will discuss how to choose the appropriate algorithm for a given problem, as well as model evaluation techniques that will help you assess the performance of your algorithms.

Understanding Algorithms in Machine Learning

In machine learning, **algorithms** are the mathematical formulas or procedures used to process data and make predictions or decisions. These algorithms allow models to learn patterns from data and generalize those patterns to new, unseen data.

The goal of any machine learning algorithm is to minimize the error in predictions or classifications. The **training** process involves feeding the algorithm data so that it can learn the relationship between the input and the output. Once trained, the model is then used to make predictions on new data.

Here's a general overview of how an algorithm works:

1. **Input data**: The algorithm is fed a dataset with input features (e.g., age, income) and corresponding output labels (e.g., whether someone will buy a product).
2. **Model training**: The algorithm analyzes the input data, identifies patterns, and adjusts its internal parameters to minimize errors.
3. **Prediction**: After training, the model is used to make predictions or classifications based on new input data.

Popular Algorithms: Linear Regression, Decision Trees, K-Nearest Neighbors, and More

There are several types of machine learning algorithms, each suited to different types of problems. Below, we will look at some of the most common algorithms.

1. Linear Regression

Linear regression is one of the simplest and most widely used algorithms for predicting continuous variables. It finds the best-fitting straight line (a linear relationship) that minimizes the error between the predicted values and the actual data.

- **Use case**: Predicting a continuous output, such as house prices based on features like size, number of rooms, and location.

Mathematical form:

The relationship between the input feature (X) and the output (Y) is modeled as: $Y=\beta_0+\beta_1 X+\epsilon$ Where:

- Y is the dependent variable (output).
- X is the independent variable (input feature).
- β_0 is the intercept.
- β_1 is the coefficient (slope of the line).
- ϵ is the error term.

Example in Python:

```python
from sklearn.linear_model import LinearRegression

# Creating a Linear Regression model
model = LinearRegression()

# Fit model on training data (X_train, y_train)
model.fit(X_train, y_train)

# Make predictions
```

```
predictions = model.predict(X_test)
```

2. Decision Trees

Decision trees are supervised learning algorithms used for both classification and regression tasks. They work by recursively splitting the data into subsets based on the feature that provides the best separation of the data, creating a tree-like structure.

- **Use case**: Predicting whether a customer will buy a product based on various features like age, income, and previous purchases.

Example in Python:

```python
python

from sklearn.tree import DecisionTreeClassifier

# Creating a decision tree model
tree_model = DecisionTreeClassifier()

# Fit model on training data
tree_model.fit(X_train, y_train)

# Make predictions
predictions = tree_model.predict(X_test)
```

3. K-Nearest Neighbors (KNN)

K-Nearest Neighbors (KNN) is a simple, instance-based learning algorithm used for both classification and regression tasks. It works by finding the k nearest data points to a given data point and making predictions based on the majority class (for classification) or average value (for regression) of those neighbors.

- **Use case**: Classifying a new customer as "high-value" or "low-value" based on their behavior compared to other customers.

Example in Python:

python

```
from          sklearn.neighbors          import
KNeighborsClassifier

# Creating a KNN model
knn_model = KNeighborsClassifier(n_neighbors=3)

# Fit model on training data
knn_model.fit(X_train, y_train)

# Make predictions
predictions = knn_model.predict(X_test)
```

4. Support Vector Machines (SVM)

Support Vector Machines (SVM) are powerful supervised learning models used for classification tasks. They work by finding the optimal hyperplane that separates data points into different classes. SVM is particularly effective in high-dimensional spaces.

- **Use case**: Classifying whether a tumor is malignant or benign based on its characteristics.

Example in Python:

```python

from sklearn.svm import SVC

# Creating an SVM model
svm_model = SVC(kernel='linear')

# Fit model on training data
svm_model.fit(X_train, y_train)

# Make predictions
predictions = svm_model.predict(X_test)
```

5. Random Forest

Random Forest is an ensemble learning method that creates multiple decision trees and combines their outputs to improve performance and avoid overfitting. It is widely used for both classification and regression problems.

- **Use case**: Predicting loan approval based on multiple factors such as credit score, income, and past debt.

Example in Python:

```python
from sklearn.ensemble import RandomForestClassifier

# Creating a random forest model
rf_model = RandomForestClassifier(n_estimators=100)

# Fit model on training data
rf_model.fit(X_train, y_train)

# Make predictions
predictions = rf_model.predict(X_test)
```

How to Select an Algorithm for Your Problem

Choosing the right machine learning algorithm depends on several factors, such as the type of problem you're trying to solve, the nature of the data, and the trade-offs you are willing to make (e.g., interpretability vs. accuracy).

Here are some general guidelines:

- **Classification vs. Regression**: Choose classification algorithms (e.g., Decision Trees, KNN, SVM) for problems where the output is categorical (e.g., "yes" or "no"), and regression algorithms (e.g., Linear Regression) when the output is continuous (e.g., house prices).
- **Linear vs. Non-Linear Models**: If you believe that the relationship between input and output is linear, go for linear models (e.g., Linear Regression). If the relationship is more complex, non-linear models like Decision Trees, Random Forest, or SVM may be better.
- **Speed vs. Accuracy**: Some algorithms, such as KNN, are computationally expensive and may not scale well for large datasets. Models like Decision Trees and Random Forests provide a good trade-off between speed and accuracy.
- **Interpretability**: If interpretability is important (e.g., in healthcare or finance), simpler models like Linear Regression or Decision Trees are easier to understand and explain. More complex models like SVM and Random Forest, though powerful, are harder to interpret.

Overview of Model Evaluation Techniques

After selecting and training a model, it's essential to evaluate its performance. There are various techniques for model evaluation, depending on the type of problem (classification or regression).

1. Classification Metrics

For classification tasks, common evaluation metrics include:

- **Accuracy**: The percentage of correctly classified instances.
- **Precision**: The proportion of true positive predictions to the total predicted positives.
- **Recall**: The proportion of true positive predictions to the total actual positives.
- **F1 Score**: The harmonic mean of precision and recall, providing a balance between them.

Example:

python

```
from sklearn.metrics import accuracy_score,
precision_score, recall_score, f1_score

accuracy = accuracy_score(y_test, predictions)
precision = precision_score(y_test, predictions)
recall = recall_score(y_test, predictions)
```

```
f1 = f1_score(y_test, predictions)

print(f"Accuracy: {accuracy}")
print(f"Precision: {precision}")
print(f"Recall: {recall}")
print(f"F1 Score: {f1}")
```

2. Regression Metrics

For regression tasks, common evaluation metrics include:

- **Mean Absolute Error (MAE)**: The average of the absolute differences between predicted and actual values.
- **Mean Squared Error (MSE)**: The average of the squared differences between predicted and actual values.
- **R-squared**: The proportion of the variance in the dependent variable that is predictable from the independent variables.

Example:

```python
from sklearn.metrics import mean_absolute_error,
mean_squared_error, r2_score

mae = mean_absolute_error(y_test, predictions)
mse = mean_squared_error(y_test, predictions)
r2 = r2_score(y_test, predictions)
```

```
print(f"MAE: {mae}")
print(f"MSE: {mse}")
print(f"R-squared: {r2}")
```

3. Cross-Validation

Cross-validation is a technique used to assess the performance of a model by dividing the data into multiple folds and training the model on different subsets of the data. This helps reduce the risk of overfitting.

Case Study: Applying Algorithms on a Dataset

Let's consider a case study where we apply some of the algorithms discussed to a dataset. In this example, we'll use a **customer churn dataset**, where we predict whether a customer will leave a company based on various features like age, usage, and payment method.

1. **Load the Dataset**:

```python
import pandas as pd

# Load the dataset
df = pd.read_csv('customer_churn.csv')
```

```
# Preview the dataset
print(df.head())
```

2. **Preprocessing**:
   - Clean missing values, encode categorical variables, and split the dataset into training and testing sets.
3. **Train Models**:
   - Train **Logistic Regression**, **Decision Tree**, and **Random Forest** models.

python

```
from        sklearn.model_selection        import
train_test_split
from          sklearn.linear_model          import
LogisticRegression
from sklearn.tree import DecisionTreeClassifier
from          sklearn.ensemble              import
RandomForestClassifier

# Split the data into features and labels
X = df.drop('Churn', axis=1)
y = df['Churn']

# Split into training and testing sets
X_train,    X_test,    y_train,    y_test    =
train_test_split(X,      y,      test_size=0.3,
random_state=42)
```

```
# Logistic Regression model
log_reg = LogisticRegression()
log_reg.fit(X_train, y_train)
log_reg_pred = log_reg.predict(X_test)


# Decision Tree model
tree_model = DecisionTreeClassifier()
tree_model.fit(X_train, y_train)
tree_pred = tree_model.predict(X_test)


# Random Forest model
rf_model = RandomForestClassifier()
rf_model.fit(X_train, y_train)
rf_pred = rf_model.predict(X_test)
```

4. **Evaluate Models**:

   o   Evaluate the models using classification metrics.

Key Takeaways

- **Machine learning algorithms** are the core of AI, allowing models to learn from data and make predictions or decisions.

- **Linear Regression**, **Decision Trees**, **KNN**, and **Random Forest** are some of the most commonly used algorithms for both classification and regression tasks.

- **Choosing the right algorithm** depends on the problem type (classification vs. regression), the nature of the data, and the need for interpretability and performance.
- **Model evaluation** techniques such as accuracy, precision, recall, F1 score, and cross-validation help assess the performance of machine learning models.

In the next chapter, we will explore **model optimization techniques** and how to fine-tune models for better performance using methods like **hyperparameter tuning** and **grid search**.

CHAPTER 7

PREPARING YOUR DATA FOR MACHINE LEARNING

In this chapter, we will discuss the crucial steps of **data preparation** for machine learning. Before applying any machine learning model, it's essential to preprocess and transform your data to ensure the best performance. We will cover **feature selection and engineering**, **normalization and standardization**, **splitting data into training and testing sets**, and how to handle **categorical and continuous data**. Additionally, we will introduce the concept of **train-test split**, which is a vital part of model evaluation.

Feature Selection and Engineering

Feature selection and engineering are key steps in preparing your data for machine learning. **Feature selection** involves choosing the most relevant features (columns) that contribute to the prediction, while **feature engineering** involves creating new features from existing data to improve model performance.

1. Feature Selection

Feature selection helps improve model accuracy by removing redundant or irrelevant data. By reducing the number of features, you can also reduce the model's complexity and overfitting.

- **Methods of feature selection**:
  - o **Correlation matrix**: Remove features that are highly correlated with one another, as they might provide redundant information.
  - o **Recursive Feature Elimination (RFE)**: This technique recursively removes the least important features based on model performance.
  - o **Feature importance**: Some models, such as decision trees, can be used to rank features by their importance.

Example:

python

```
import pandas as pd
import seaborn as sns

# Calculate correlation matrix
corr_matrix = df.corr()

# Visualize the correlation matrix
```

```
sns.heatmap(corr_matrix,                    annot=True,
cmap='coolwarm', fmt='.2f')
```

2. Feature Engineering

Feature engineering is the process of transforming raw data into features that make machine learning algorithms work better. It involves:

- **Creating new features**: For example, you could create an "age group" feature from the "age" feature (e.g., 0-18, 19-35, etc.).
- **Handling missing values**: You might create a new feature indicating whether a value was missing for a particular row.

Example:

Creating a new feature, "Age Group":

```
python
```

```
df['Age Group'] = pd.cut(df['Age'], bins=[0, 18,
35, 50, 100], labels=['0-18', '19-35', '36-50',
'50+'])
```

Normalization and Standardization

Normalization and standardization are techniques used to scale your data, making sure that no single feature dominates the learning process.

1. Normalization

Normalization rescales data into a specific range, typically [0, 1]. This is particularly useful for algorithms like **K-Nearest Neighbors (KNN)** and **Neural Networks**, which rely on the scale of input features.

- **Formula**:

  Xnorm=X−XminXmax−XminX_{norm} = \frac{X - X_{min}}{X_{max} - X_{min}}Xnorm=Xmax−XminX−Xmin Where XXX is the original value, XminX_{min}Xmin is the minimum value in the feature, and XmaxX_{max}Xmax is the maximum value in the feature.

Example in Python:

python

```
from sklearn.preprocessing import MinMaxScaler

# Initializing the Normalizer
```

```
scaler = MinMaxScaler()

# Applying normalization
df[['Age',          'Income']]          =
scaler.fit_transform(df[['Age', 'Income']])
```

2. Standardization

Standardization transforms data into a distribution with a mean of 0 and a standard deviation of 1. This is useful for algorithms that assume the data is normally distributed (e.g., **Linear Regression**, **Logistic Regression**).

- **Formula**: $Xstd=X-\mu\sigma X_{std} = \frac{X - \mu}{\sigma} Xstd=\sigma X-\mu$ Where XXX is the original value, $\mu\backslash mu\mu$ is the mean, and $\sigma\backslash sigma\sigma$ is the standard deviation.

Example in Python:

```python
python

from sklearn.preprocessing import StandardScaler

# Initializing the StandardScaler
scaler = StandardScaler()

# Applying standardization
df[['Age',          'Income']]          =
scaler.fit_transform(df[['Age', 'Income']])
```

Splitting Data into Training and Testing Sets

To evaluate the performance of your machine learning model, you need to split your dataset into **training** and **testing** sets. This allows you to train the model on one subset of data and test its performance on another subset that the model hasn't seen during training.

1. Train-Test Split

A common approach is to split the data into two sets:

- **Training set**: The data used to train the machine learning model.
- **Testing set**: The data used to evaluate the model's performance.

The typical split ratio is 70-30 or 80-20, where 70% (or 80%) of the data is used for training, and the remaining 30% (or 20%) is used for testing.

Example in Python:

```python

from        sklearn.model_selection       import
train_test_split

# Splitting the data
```

```
X_train,    X_test,    y_train,    y_test    =
train_test_split(df[['Age',          'Income']],
df['Churn'], test_size=0.3, random_state=42)
```

```
# Check the shape of the resulting datasets
print(X_train.shape, X_test.shape)
```

This code splits the features (df[['Age', 'Income']]) and the target (df['Churn']) into training and testing sets. The test_size parameter specifies the proportion of data to allocate to the test set (30% in this case).

2. Stratified Sampling

When you have **imbalanced classes** in your target variable (e.g., more "No" churns than "Yes" churns), it's important to split the data in such a way that the class distribution is similar in both the training and testing sets. This can be done using **stratified sampling**.

Example in Python:

```python
```

```
X_train,    X_test,    y_train,    y_test    =
train_test_split(df[['Age',          'Income']],
df['Churn'],                    test_size=0.3,
stratify=df['Churn'], random_state=42)
```

This ensures that both the training and testing sets have the same distribution of the target variable.

Dealing with Categorical and Continuous Data

Data can be classified into two broad types: **categorical data** and **continuous data**. Handling these two types of data appropriately is crucial for machine learning models.

1. Categorical Data

Categorical data represents categories or groups. Examples include gender, product types, or countries. Machine learning models typically cannot work with raw categorical data directly, so we need to **encode** it into numerical values.

- **One-Hot Encoding**: This method creates a binary (0 or 1) column for each category in the original feature.
    - **Example**: For the "Gender" column with values "Male" and "Female", one-hot encoding will create two columns: "Gender_Male" and "Gender_Female".

Example in Python:

```
python
```

```
df   =   pd.get_dummies(df,   columns=['Gender'],
drop_first=True)
```

- **Label Encoding**: This method assigns a unique integer to each category.
    - **Example**: "Male" = 0, "Female" = 1.

Example in Python:

```python
python

from sklearn.preprocessing import LabelEncoder

# Label encoding for the "Gender" column
le = LabelEncoder()
df['Gender'] = le.fit_transform(df['Gender'])
```

2. Continuous Data

Continuous data represents numerical values, such as age, income, or temperature. Continuous features are often used directly in machine learning models after being preprocessed (e.g., normalization or standardization).

Introduction to Train-Test Split in Python

As mentioned earlier, splitting the data into training and testing sets is a critical step in machine learning. **train_test_split** from **scikit-learn** is a function that automates this process.

Basic Syntax:

```python
```

```python
from        sklearn.model_selection        import
train_test_split

# Splitting the data
X_train,    X_test,    y_train,    y_test    =
train_test_split(features,                target,
test_size=0.3, random_state=42)
```

- **features**: The input data (independent variables or predictors).
- **target**: The output data (dependent variable or label).
- **test_size**: The proportion of data to include in the test set (e.g., 0.3 for 30%).
- **random_state**: A seed value to ensure reproducibility.

Stratified Split for Classification Problems:

For classification problems with imbalanced datasets, you should use **stratified sampling** to ensure that the distribution of classes is similar in both the training and testing sets.

```python
```

```python
X_train,    X_test,    y_train,    y_test    =
train_test_split(features,                target,
test_size=0.3, stratify=target, random_state=42)
```

Key Takeaways

- **Feature selection and engineering** are important steps to ensure that the machine learning model focuses on relevant features and creates new features to improve performance.

- **Normalization** and **standardization** help scale the data, ensuring that no single feature dominates the learning process.

- **Splitting the data into training and testing sets** allows you to evaluate the model's performance on unseen data, which is crucial for avoiding overfitting.

- **Categorical data** needs to be encoded into numerical values using methods like one-hot encoding or label encoding, while **continuous data** can typically be used directly after scaling.

- The **train-test split** is a fundamental concept in machine learning, and using it correctly helps in validating the model's generalization ability.

In the next chapter, we will explore how to apply machine learning algorithms to the preprocessed data and begin building models using both **supervised** and **unsupervised learning** techniques.

CHAPTER 8

BUILDING YOUR FIRST AI MODEL

In this chapter, we will guide you through the process of building your first AI model using **scikit-learn**, one of the most popular machine learning libraries in Python. We will walk you through the steps of building a simple **linear regression model**, training and testing the model, and evaluating its performance using metrics like **accuracy**, **precision**, and **recall**. Finally, we will apply these concepts to a **case study** where we predict house prices based on different features using linear regression.

Introduction to scikit-learn

scikit-learn is a Python library that provides simple and efficient tools for data mining and machine learning. It is built on top of other scientific libraries such as **NumPy**, **SciPy**, and **matplotlib**, and is designed to work seamlessly with Python's other data manipulation tools like **pandas**.

scikit-learn provides various tools for:

- **Supervised learning** (classification, regression)

96

- **Unsupervised learning** (clustering, dimensionality reduction)
- **Model selection** (cross-validation, hyperparameter tuning)
- **Preprocessing** (scaling, encoding)
- **Evaluation** (metrics for classification and regression)

To install scikit-learn, use the following:

bash

```
pip install scikit-learn
```

Building a Simple Linear Regression Model

Linear regression is one of the most fundamental algorithms in machine learning and is used for predicting continuous values. In linear regression, the model tries to fit a straight line (a linear relationship) between the input features and the target variable.

1. Preparing the Data

Before building the model, we need to load and prepare the data. Let's use a dataset that predicts house prices based on features such as size, number of rooms, and location. We will use **pandas** to load the data and split it into input features (X) and target labels (y).

Example in Python:

```python
python

import pandas as pd

# Load the dataset (assuming it's in CSV format)
df = pd.read_csv('house_prices.csv')

# Preview the dataset
print(df.head())

# Define the input features (X) and target (y)
X = df[['Size', 'Bedrooms', 'Location']]
y = df['Price']
```

2. Splitting the Data

We will split the data into training and testing sets. This allows us to train the model on one portion of the data and evaluate its performance on another portion that it hasn't seen during training.

Example in Python:

```python
python

from        sklearn.model_selection        import
train_test_split
```

```
# Split the data into training and testing sets
(80% for training, 20% for testing)
X_train,    X_test,    y_train,    y_test    =
train_test_split(X,    y,    test_size=0.2,
random_state=42)


# Check the shape of the resulting datasets
print(X_train.shape, X_test.shape)
```

3. Building the Linear Regression Model

Now that the data is prepared, we can create the linear regression model using scikit-learn's **LinearRegression** class.

Example in Python:

```python
python


from        sklearn.linear_model        import
LinearRegression


# Initialize the model
model = LinearRegression()


# Train the model using the training data
model.fit(X_train, y_train)
```

At this point, the model has learned the relationship between the features (Size, Bedrooms, Location) and the target variable (Price).

Training and Testing the Model

Once the model is trained, we can use the test set to make predictions and evaluate how well the model performs.

1. Making Predictions

Using the trained model, we can make predictions on the test data (X_test), which represents data the model hasn't seen before.

Example in Python:

python

```
# Make predictions on the test set
y_pred = model.predict(X_test)

# Display the predicted values
print(y_pred)
```

2. Evaluating Model Performance

To assess how well the model has performed, we use evaluation metrics. For regression tasks like predicting house prices, common metrics include:

- **R-squared (R^2)**: This measures how well the model explains the variance in the data. The value ranges from 0 to 1, where 1 means the model perfectly explains the variance.

- **Mean Absolute Error (MAE)**: The average of the absolute differences between predicted and actual values.
- **Mean Squared Error (MSE)**: The average of the squared differences between predicted and actual values.

We can evaluate the model using scikit-learn's built-in functions.

Example in Python:

python

```
from sklearn.metrics import mean_absolute_error,
mean_squared_error, r2_score

# Calculate the evaluation metrics
mae = mean_absolute_error(y_test, y_pred)
mse = mean_squared_error(y_test, y_pred)
r2 = r2_score(y_test, y_pred)

# Display the results
print(f"Mean Absolute Error: {mae}")
print(f"Mean Squared Error: {mse}")
print(f"R-squared: {r2}")
```

3. Interpreting the Results

- **R-squared (R²)**: A value closer to 1 indicates that the model does a good job of explaining the variance in the target variable.
- **Mean Absolute Error (MAE)**: This gives you the average error between predicted and actual values. A lower MAE indicates better model performance.
- **Mean Squared Error (MSE)**: Similar to MAE, but MSE penalizes larger errors more heavily due to the squared term.

Case Study: Predicting House Prices with Linear Regression

To put all of these concepts into practice, let's consider a real-world dataset for predicting house prices. In this case study, we'll use **linear regression** to predict the price of a house based on features such as the number of rooms, size, and location.

Step 1: Load the Data

For the case study, let's assume we have a dataset `house_prices.csv` with the following columns:

- **Size**: The size of the house in square feet.
- **Bedrooms**: The number of bedrooms.
- **Location**: The location of the house.

- **Price**: The target variable, which is the price of the house.

python

```
import pandas as pd

# Load the dataset
df = pd.read_csv('house_prices.csv')

# Preview the dataset
print(df.head())
```

Step 2: Preprocessing the Data

- Handle missing values if any.
- Encode categorical data (e.g., Location) using **One-Hot Encoding**.
- Split the data into features and target.

python

```
# Fill missing values for simplicity
df = df.fillna(df.mean())

# One-hot encode the 'Location' column
df = pd.get_dummies(df, columns=['Location'],
drop_first=True)

# Define input features (X) and target variable
(y)
```

```
X = df[['Size', 'Bedrooms', 'Location_New York',
'Location_Los Angeles']]
y = df['Price']
```

Step 3: Split the Data

We will split the data into training and testing sets.

```
python
```

```
from         sklearn.model_selection      import
train_test_split

# Split the data into 80% training and 20% testing
X_train,    X_test,    y_train,    y_test    =
train_test_split(X,    y,    test_size=0.2,
random_state=42)

# Check the shape of the training and testing
sets
print(X_train.shape, X_test.shape)
```

Step 4: Train the Model

Now, let's create and train our linear regression model.

```
python
```

```
from         sklearn.linear_model        import
LinearRegression
```

```
# Initialize the model
model = LinearRegression()

# Train the model on the training data
model.fit(X_train, y_train)
```

Step 5: Make Predictions and Evaluate the Model

Next, we will make predictions on the test data and evaluate the model's performance.

python

```
from sklearn.metrics import mean_absolute_error,
mean_squared_error, r2_score

# Make predictions on the test data
y_pred = model.predict(X_test)

# Evaluate the model's performance
mae = mean_absolute_error(y_test, y_pred)
mse = mean_squared_error(y_test, y_pred)
r2 = r2_score(y_test, y_pred)

# Display the results
print(f"Mean Absolute Error: {mae}")
print(f"Mean Squared Error: {mse}")
print(f"R-squared: {r2}")
```

Step 6: Interpret the Results

- If the **R-squared** value is close to 1, the model is doing a good job of predicting house prices.
- **MAE** and **MSE** provide additional insight into the accuracy of the model's predictions.

Key Takeaways

- **scikit-learn** is an essential Python library for building machine learning models. It provides an easy-to-use interface for training, evaluating, and testing models.
- **Linear regression** is one of the simplest algorithms for predicting continuous values, and it works by fitting a line through the data to minimize errors.
- **Model evaluation** is crucial for understanding the effectiveness of your AI model. Use metrics like **R-squared**, **MAE**, and **MSE** to assess model performance.
- In the case study, we demonstrated how to use **linear regression** to predict house prices, from preprocessing the data to evaluating the model's performance.

In the next chapter, we will explore more advanced machine learning models and techniques, including **decision trees**, **random forests**, and **support vector machines (SVM)**.

CHAPTER 9

CLASSIFICATION ALGORITHMS IN AI

In this chapter, we will explore **classification problems** in AI and machine learning. Classification is a type of supervised learning where the goal is to predict the category or class label of an object based on its features. We will dive into several popular classification algorithms like **Logistic Regression**, **Decision Trees**, **K-Nearest Neighbors (k-NN)**, and **Support Vector Machines (SVM)**. Additionally, we will discuss how to evaluate classification models using metrics like the **confusion matrix** and the **ROC curve**. We will conclude the chapter with a **case study** on **classifying emails as spam or not spam**.

Introduction to Classification Problems

In a **classification problem**, the goal is to predict a discrete label or category for an input data point. This is in contrast to **regression problems**, where the goal is to predict continuous values. Common examples of classification tasks include:

- **Email spam detection**: Classifying emails as "spam" or "not spam."

- **Image recognition**: Classifying images of animals as "cat", "dog", or "bird."
- **Medical diagnosis**: Classifying whether a patient has a certain disease or not.

In machine learning, the model learns from labeled data (where each input comes with a corresponding label) and uses this information to classify new, unseen data.

Understanding Algorithms: Logistic Regression, Decision Trees, k-NN, and SVM

1. Logistic Regression

Logistic Regression is one of the simplest and most widely used algorithms for binary classification (i.e., classifying data into two classes). Despite its name, logistic regression is a classification algorithm rather than a regression one. It models the probability of a class belonging to a particular category based on input features.

The algorithm uses the **sigmoid function** (also called the logistic function) to transform the predicted output into a probability value between 0 and 1:

$$\text{Sigmoid}(z) = \frac{1}{1 + e^{-z}}$$

where zzz is the linear combination of input features.

Example in Python:

python

```
from        sklearn.linear_model        import
LogisticRegression

# Initialize the logistic regression model
model = LogisticRegression()

# Train the model on the training data
model.fit(X_train, y_train)

# Make predictions on the test set
y_pred = model.predict(X_test)
```

2. Decision Trees

Decision Trees are versatile classifiers that work by splitting the data based on feature values, creating a tree-like structure where each internal node represents a decision rule based on a feature, and each leaf node represents a class label.

- **Advantages**: Easy to understand and interpret, no need for feature scaling.
- **Disadvantages**: Prone to overfitting, especially with deep trees.

109

Example in Python:

```python

from sklearn.tree import DecisionTreeClassifier

# Initialize the decision tree model
tree_model = DecisionTreeClassifier()

# Train the model
tree_model.fit(X_train, y_train)

# Make predictions
y_pred = tree_model.predict(X_test)
```

3. K-Nearest Neighbors (k-NN)

K-Nearest Neighbors (k-NN) is a simple, instance-based learning algorithm where the prediction for a new data point is based on the majority class of its k nearest neighbors in the feature space. The "k" parameter defines how many neighbors the algorithm looks at when making a decision.

- **Advantages**: Simple to understand and implement, no training required.
- **Disadvantages**: Computationally expensive, especially with large datasets.

Example in Python:

```
python

from            sklearn.neighbors            import
KNeighborsClassifier

# Initialize the k-NN model
knn_model = KNeighborsClassifier(n_neighbors=3)

# Train the model
knn_model.fit(X_train, y_train)

# Make predictions
y_pred = knn_model.predict(X_test)
```

4. Support Vector Machines (SVM)

Support Vector Machines (SVM) are powerful classifiers that work by finding the optimal hyperplane that separates data points into different classes. SVMs are especially effective in high-dimensional spaces and can be used for both linear and non-linear classification tasks by applying kernel functions.

- **Advantages**: Effective in high-dimensional spaces, robust to overfitting.
- **Disadvantages**: Requires careful tuning of hyperparameters, computationally expensive for large datasets.

Example in Python:

```python
from sklearn.svm import SVC

# Initialize the SVM model
svm_model = SVC(kernel='linear')

# Train the model
svm_model.fit(X_train, y_train)

# Make predictions
y_pred = svm_model.predict(X_test)
```

Working with Classification Metrics: Confusion Matrix, ROC Curve

To evaluate the performance of classification models, we use various metrics. The most common ones include the **confusion matrix**, **accuracy**, **precision**, **recall**, and the **ROC curve**.

1. Confusion Matrix

The **confusion matrix** is a table that is used to evaluate the performance of a classification model. It compares the actual target values with those predicted by the model. It helps us understand the types of errors the model is making.

The confusion matrix contains the following elements:

- **True Positives (TP)**: Correctly predicted positive instances.

- **True Negatives (TN)**: Correctly predicted negative instances.

- **False Positives (FP)**: Incorrectly predicted positive instances (Type I error).

- **False Negatives (FN)**: Incorrectly predicted negative instances (Type II error).

Example in Python:

python

```
from sklearn.metrics import confusion_matrix

# Generate the confusion matrix
cm = confusion_matrix(y_test, y_pred)

print("Confusion Matrix:")
print(cm)
```

2. Accuracy, Precision, Recall, and F1 Score

- **Accuracy**: The ratio of correct predictions to the total number of predictions.

Accuracy=TP+TNTP+TN+FP+FN\text{Accuracy} = \frac{TP + TN}{TP + TN + FP + FN}Accuracy=TP+TN+FNTP+TN

113

- **Precision**: The ratio of correctly predicted positive observations to the total predicted positives.

Precision=TPTP+FP\text{Precision} = \frac{TP}{TP + FP}Precision=TP+FPTP

- **Recall (Sensitivity)**: The ratio of correctly predicted positive observations to all observations in the actual positive class.

Recall=TPTP+FN\text{Recall} = \frac{TP}{TP + FN}Recall=TP+FNTP

- **F1 Score**: The harmonic mean of precision and recall. It's a good metric when you need a balance between precision and recall.

F1=2×Precision×RecallPrecision+RecallF1 = 2 \times \frac{\text{Precision} \times \text{Recall}}{\text{Precision} + \text{Recall}}F1=2×Precision+RecallPrecision×Recall

Example in Python:

```python
from sklearn.metrics import accuracy_score, precision_score, recall_score, f1_score
```

```
accuracy = accuracy_score(y_test, y_pred)
precision = precision_score(y_test, y_pred)
recall = recall_score(y_test, y_pred)
f1 = f1_score(y_test, y_pred)

print(f"Accuracy: {accuracy}")
print(f"Precision: {precision}")
print(f"Recall: {recall}")
print(f"F1 Score: {f1}")
```

3. ROC Curve and AUC

The **Receiver Operating Characteristic (ROC) curve** is a graphical representation of the model's ability to distinguish between classes. It plots the **True Positive Rate (TPR)** against the **False Positive Rate (FPR)** at various classification thresholds.

- **Area Under the Curve (AUC)**: The AUC score tells you how well the model is performing. A score of 1 represents perfect classification, and 0.5 represents random guessing.

Example in Python:

```python
python

from sklearn.metrics import roc_curve, auc
import matplotlib.pyplot as plt
```

```
# Calculate ROC curve
fpr,      tpr,      _      =      roc_curve(y_test,
model.predict_proba(X_test)[:,1])
roc_auc = auc(fpr, tpr)


# Plot ROC curve
plt.figure()
plt.plot(fpr,  tpr,  color='darkorange',  lw=2,
label='ROC curve (area = %0.2f)' % roc_auc)
plt.plot([0,  1],  [0,  1],  color='navy',  lw=2,
linestyle='--')
plt.xlabel('False Positive Rate')
plt.ylabel('True Positive Rate')
plt.title('Receiver Operating Characteristic')
plt.legend(loc="lower right")
plt.show()
```

Case Study: Classifying Emails as Spam or Not Spam

In this case study, we will classify emails as either **spam** or **not spam** based on various features like the presence of specific words, email length, or sender's domain. We will apply the **Logistic Regression** algorithm to this problem.

Step 1: Load the Dataset

Let's assume we have a dataset emails.csv with the following columns:

- **Text**: The content of the email.
- **Label**: The label indicating whether the email is spam (1) or not spam (0).

```python
import pandas as pd

# Load the dataset
df = pd.read_csv('emails.csv')

# Preview the dataset
print(df.head())
```

Step 2: Preprocess the Data

- **Convert text to numeric features** using **TF-IDF** or **Count Vectorization**.
- **Split the data** into training and testing sets.

```python
from sklearn.model_selection import train_test_split
from sklearn.feature_extraction.text import TfidfVectorizer

# Convert text to TF-IDF features
vectorizer = TfidfVectorizer(stop_words='english')
```

```
X = vectorizer.fit_transform(df['Text'])
```

```
# Target variable
y = df['Label']
```

```
# Split the data into training and testing sets
X_train,    X_test,    y_train,    y_test    =
train_test_split(X,       y,       test_size=0.2,
random_state=42)
```

Step 3: Train the Logistic Regression Model

```
python
```

```
from         sklearn.linear_model          import
LogisticRegression
```

```
# Initialize the model
model = LogisticRegression()
```

```
# Train the model
model.fit(X_train, y_train)
```

Step 4: Evaluate the Model

Use the **confusion matrix, precision, recall,** and **ROC curve** to evaluate the performance.

```
python
```

```
from  sklearn.metrics  import  confusion_matrix,
precision_score, recall_score, f1_score
```

```
# Make predictions
y_pred = model.predict(X_test)

# Evaluate the model
print("Confusion Matrix:")
print(confusion_matrix(y_test, y_pred))

print(f"Precision:       {precision_score(y_test,
y_pred)}")
print(f"Recall: {recall_score(y_test, y_pred)}")
print(f"F1 Score: {f1_score(y_test, y_pred)}")
```

Key Takeaways

- **Classification algorithms** are used to predict categorical outcomes, and they are a key part of many AI applications such as spam detection, image classification, and medical diagnosis.

- **Popular algorithms** like **Logistic Regression**, **Decision Trees**, **K-NN**, and **SVM** have different strengths and weaknesses depending on the dataset and problem.

- **Performance metrics** such as **accuracy**, **precision**, **recall**, and the **ROC curve** help you assess how well a model is performing.

119

- In the **case study**, we applied **Logistic Regression** to classify emails as spam or not spam, using text data and evaluation metrics to assess the model's performance.

In the next chapter, we will explore more advanced classification techniques and optimization methods to improve model performance.

CHAPTER 10

REGRESSION MODELS IN AI

In this chapter, we will dive into **regression problems** in AI, which are used to predict continuous values. Regression is one of the most commonly applied techniques in machine learning and is the foundation for many predictive tasks. We will explore popular regression algorithms such as **Linear Regression** and **Decision Tree Regression**, how to evaluate regression models using metrics like **R-squared** and **Mean Squared Error (MSE)**, and end with a **case study** on predicting sales based on advertising spend.

Introduction to Regression Problems

Regression problems are a type of **supervised learning** where the goal is to predict a continuous numerical value based on input features. In contrast to **classification problems**, where the output is categorical, regression models predict real values.

Some typical regression problems include:

- Predicting house prices based on various features (e.g., square footage, number of rooms).

- Predicting sales revenue based on advertising spend and other factors.
- Forecasting stock prices based on historical data.

In machine learning, we train a regression model on data that contains both the **input features** (independent variables) and the **target variable** (dependent variable), which is the continuous value we want to predict.

Understanding Regression Algorithms: Linear Regression, Decision Tree Regression

1. Linear Regression

Linear regression is one of the simplest and most widely used algorithms in machine learning. It establishes a linear relationship between the independent variables (features) and the dependent variable (target).

In **simple linear regression**, the relationship between a single input feature XXX and the output YYY is modeled as:

$Y=\beta 0+\beta 1X+\epsilon Y = \beta\_0 + \beta\_1X + \epsilon Y=\beta 0+\beta 1X+\epsilon$

Where:

- YYY is the predicted output (target).
- $\beta 0$\beta_0$\beta 0$ is the intercept (bias).

- $\beta1\backslash beta\_1\beta1$ is the coefficient (slope) of the input feature.
- $\epsilon\backslash epsilon\epsilon$ is the error term.

Multiple linear regression extends this to multiple input features, where the relationship is modeled as:

$Y=\beta0+\beta1X1+\beta2X2+\cdots+\beta nXn+\epsilon Y = \backslash beta\_0 + \backslash beta\_1X\_1 + \backslash beta\_2X\_2 + \backslash dots + \backslash beta\_nX\_n + \backslash epsilon Y=\beta0+\beta1X1+\beta2X2+\cdots+\beta nXn+\epsilon$

Where $X1,X2,\ldots,XnX\_1, X\_2, \backslash dots, X\_nX1,X2,\ldots,Xn$ are the multiple input features.

Example in Python:

```python
from        sklearn.linear_model        import
LinearRegression

# Initialize the linear regression model
model = LinearRegression()

# Train the model on the training data
model.fit(X_train, y_train)

# Make predictions on the test set
y_pred = model.predict(X_test)
```

2. Decision Tree Regression

A **decision tree regression** model works by partitioning the data into different subsets based on feature values and making predictions based on the average of the target variable in each partition. This method works well when the relationship between features and the target is non-linear.

Decision trees for regression create a tree structure where:

- Each internal node represents a feature and a decision rule.
- Each leaf node contains the predicted value for the target variable.

Advantages:

- Can handle non-linear relationships.
- No need for feature scaling.

Disadvantages:

- Prone to overfitting, especially with deeper trees.

Example in Python:

python

```
from sklearn.tree import DecisionTreeRegressor
```

```
# Initialize the decision tree regressor model
tree_model = DecisionTreeRegressor()

# Train the model
tree_model.fit(X_train, y_train)

# Make predictions
y_pred = tree_model.predict(X_test)
```

Model Evaluation: R-squared, Mean Squared Error (MSE)

Once a regression model is trained, it's important to evaluate how well it performs. There are several metrics used to assess the accuracy and performance of regression models.

1. R-squared (R^2)

R-squared is a measure of how well the model explains the variance in the target variable. It ranges from 0 to 1, where:

- An R^2 value of 1 means the model perfectly predicts the target variable.
- An R^2 value of 0 means the model explains none of the variance.

The formula for R^2 is:

R2=1−∑i(yi−yi^)2∑i(yi−y⁻)2R^2 = 1 - \frac{\sum_{i}(y_i - \hat{y_i})^2}{\sum_{i}(y_i - \bar{y})^2}R2=1−∑i(yi−y⁻)2∑i(yi−yi^)2

Where:

- yiy_iyi is the actual value.
- yi^\hat{y_i}yi^ is the predicted value.
- y⁻\bar{y}y⁻ is the mean of the actual values.

Example in Python:

```python
from sklearn.metrics import r2_score

# Calculate R-squared
r2 = r2_score(y_test, y_pred)
print(f"R-squared: {r2}")
```

2. Mean Squared Error (MSE)

Mean Squared Error (MSE) measures the average of the squared differences between the predicted and actual values. The lower the MSE, the better the model's predictions.

The formula for MSE is:

MSE=1n∑i(yi−yi^)2MSE = \frac{1}{n} \sum_{i}(y_i - \hat{y_i})^2MSE=n1i∑(yi−yi^)2

126

Where:

- y_i iyi is the actual value.
- $\hat{y_i}$ \hat{y_i}yi^ is the predicted value.
- $n$nn is the number of data points.

Example in Python:

```python
from sklearn.metrics import mean_squared_error

# Calculate MSE
mse = mean_squared_error(y_test, y_pred)
print(f"Mean Squared Error: {mse}")
```

Case Study: Predicting Sales Based on Advertising Spend

Let's apply what we've learned in this chapter with a **case study**: Predicting **sales** based on **advertising spend** using **linear regression**. In this case, we'll use a dataset that contains two columns:

- **Advertising Spend**: The amount of money spent on advertising (in thousands of dollars).
- **Sales**: The number of units sold.

Step 1: Load the Dataset

For simplicity, let's assume the data is stored in a CSV file called `sales_data.csv`.

```python
import pandas as pd

# Load the dataset
df = pd.read_csv('sales_data.csv')

# Preview the dataset
print(df.head())
```

The dataset might look like this:

Advertising Spend	Sales
50	200
60	220
70	250
80	280
90	310

Step 2: Split the Data

We'll split the data into training and testing sets.

python

```
from        sklearn.model_selection        import
train_test_split

# Define input features (X) and target variable
(y)
X = df[['Advertising Spend']]
y = df['Sales']

# Split the data into training and testing sets
X_train,    X_test,    y_train,    y_test    =
train_test_split(X,     y,      test_size=0.2,
random_state=42)

print(X_train.shape, X_test.shape)
```

Step 3: Build and Train the Linear Regression Model

python

```
from        sklearn.linear_model        import
LinearRegression

# Initialize the model
model = LinearRegression()
```

```
# Train the model
model.fit(X_train, y_train)
```

Step 4: Make Predictions and Evaluate the Model

Now, we will use the model to make predictions on the test set and evaluate its performance.

python

```
# Make predictions
y_pred = model.predict(X_test)

# Evaluate the model using R-squared and MSE
from    sklearn.metrics    import    r2_score,
mean_squared_error

# R-squared
r2 = r2_score(y_test, y_pred)
print(f"R-squared: {r2}")

# MSE
mse = mean_squared_error(y_test, y_pred)
print(f"Mean Squared Error: {mse}")
```

Step 5: Interpret the Results

- **R-squared**: This tells us how well our model explains the variance in the sales data. A value close to 1 means that the model does a good job of predicting sales based on advertising spend.

- **Mean Squared Error (MSE)**: The lower the MSE, the better the model's predictions.

Key Takeaways

- **Regression** is used to predict continuous values based on input features.
- **Linear regression** is the simplest regression algorithm, where the relationship between the features and target variable is modeled as a straight line.
- **Decision Tree Regression** is a more flexible approach that works well when the relationship between features and the target is non-linear.
- **R-squared** and **MSE** are key metrics used to evaluate regression models.
- In the **case study**, we used linear regression to predict sales based on advertising spend, trained the model, made predictions, and evaluated its performance using R-squared and MSE.

In the next chapter, we will explore advanced regression techniques such as **Random Forest Regression** and **Support Vector Regression** for handling more complex regression problems.

CHAPTER 11

UNSUPERVISED LEARNING AND CLUSTERING

In this chapter, we will explore **unsupervised learning**, which is a type of machine learning where the model is trained on data without labeled outputs. We will focus on **clustering algorithms** like **K-means**, **hierarchical clustering**, and **DBSCAN**. Additionally, we will discuss **dimensionality reduction techniques** such as **Principal Component Analysis (PCA)** to reduce the complexity of data. Finally, we will conclude with a **case study** on **customer segmentation for marketing**, which will help illustrate how these techniques are applied in real-world scenarios.

What is Unsupervised Learning?

In **unsupervised learning**, the model is given input data without labeled outputs. Unlike **supervised learning**, where the data comes with known labels (e.g., "cat" or "dog"), unsupervised learning algorithms try to find hidden patterns or relationships in the data on their own.

The two main types of unsupervised learning tasks are:

1. **Clustering**: Grouping similar data points together based on shared characteristics.

2. **Dimensionality Reduction**: Reducing the number of features (or dimensions) in the dataset while retaining important information.

Unsupervised learning is often used for:

- **Customer segmentation**: Grouping customers based on purchasing behavior or demographics.

- **Anomaly detection**: Identifying unusual patterns or outliers in the data.

- **Market basket analysis**: Discovering relationships between products purchased together.

Clustering Algorithms: K-means, Hierarchical Clustering, DBSCAN

Clustering is one of the most common techniques in unsupervised learning. It involves grouping similar data points together into clusters, where data points within a cluster are more similar to each other than to those in other clusters.

1. K-means Clustering

K-means clustering is a popular clustering algorithm that partitions the data into K clusters, where each cluster is represented by the mean (centroid) of the data points assigned to it. The algorithm iteratively assigns each data point to the nearest centroid and recalculates the centroids until convergence.

- **How K-means works**:
    1. Choose K initial centroids (either randomly or by some heuristic).
    2. Assign each data point to the nearest centroid.
    3. Update the centroids by calculating the mean of all data points in each cluster.
    4. Repeat steps 2 and 3 until the centroids no longer change.

Example in Python:

```python

from sklearn.cluster import KMeans
import matplotlib.pyplot as plt

# Create the KMeans model with K=3 clusters
kmeans = KMeans(n_clusters=3)

# Fit the model on data (X_train)
kmeans.fit(X_train)

# Get the cluster labels for each data point
labels = kmeans.predict(X_test)

# Plot the clusters
```

```
plt.scatter(X_test[:,    0],    X_test[:,    1],
c=labels, cmap='viridis')
plt.title('K-means Clustering')
plt.show()
```

2. Hierarchical Clustering

Hierarchical clustering is a method of cluster analysis that builds a tree of clusters (called a **dendrogram**) by either:

- **Agglomerative**: Starting with individual points and progressively merging them into clusters.
- **Divisive**: Starting with all data points in one cluster and progressively splitting them.

This method doesn't require specifying the number of clusters beforehand. Instead, a **cut-off** is made in the dendrogram to decide the number of clusters.

- **Agglomerative Hierarchical Clustering** is the most common approach, where the algorithm starts by treating each data point as its own cluster and iteratively merges the closest clusters.

Example in Python:

```
python
```

```
from        sklearn.cluster        import
AgglomerativeClustering
```

```
import seaborn as sns

# Create the Agglomerative Clustering model
hierarchical_model                           =
AgglomerativeClustering(n_clusters=3)

# Fit the model
labels = hierarchical_model.fit_predict(X_train)

# Plot the clusters
sns.scatterplot(x=X_train[:,  0],  y=X_train[:,
1], hue=labels, palette="viridis")
plt.title('Hierarchical Clustering')
plt.show()
```

3. DBSCAN (Density-Based Spatial Clustering of Applications with Noise)

DBSCAN is a density-based clustering algorithm that groups together points that are closely packed and marks points in low-density regions as outliers. Unlike K-means, DBSCAN doesn't require the number of clusters to be specified beforehand and can handle clusters of arbitrary shapes.

- **How DBSCAN works**:
    1. A core point is defined as a point that has at least a minimum number of neighbors within a given radius.

2. Points that are reachable from the core points are included in the same cluster.

3. Noise points are those that don't belong to any cluster.

Example in Python:

```python
python

from sklearn.cluster import DBSCAN
import numpy as np

# Create the DBSCAN model
dbscan = DBSCAN(eps=0.5, min_samples=5)

# Fit the model
labels = dbscan.fit_predict(X_train)

# Plot the clusters
plt.scatter(X_train[:,    0],    X_train[:,    1],
c=labels, cmap='viridis')
plt.title('DBSCAN Clustering')
plt.show()
```

Dimensionality Reduction Techniques: PCA (Principal Component Analysis)

Principal Component Analysis (PCA) is a technique for reducing the number of features (or dimensions) in a dataset while preserving as much variance (information) as possible. This is useful when you have datasets with many features, which can be computationally expensive or difficult to interpret.

PCA works by finding the **principal components** (directions of maximum variance) and projecting the data onto these components, thus reducing the number of dimensions.

How PCA Works:

1. Standardize the data (mean of 0, variance of 1).
2. Compute the covariance matrix of the data.
3. Find the eigenvectors (principal components) and eigenvalues of the covariance matrix.
4. Sort the eigenvectors by eigenvalue in descending order and select the top k eigenvectors.
5. Project the data onto these k eigenvectors to reduce dimensionality.

Example in Python:

python

```
from sklearn.decomposition import PCA
import matplotlib.pyplot as plt

# Standardize the data
from sklearn.preprocessing import StandardScaler
X_scaled                                        =
StandardScaler().fit_transform(X_train)

# Apply PCA to reduce the data to 2 components
pca = PCA(n_components=2)
X_pca = pca.fit_transform(X_scaled)

# Plot the data
plt.scatter(X_pca[:, 0], X_pca[:, 1])
plt.title('PCA (2 components)')
plt.show()
```

Case Study: Customer Segmentation for Marketing

In this case study, we will use **clustering algorithms** to perform **customer segmentation** based on purchasing behavior. Customer segmentation is crucial for targeted marketing, where businesses aim to group customers into distinct segments based on similar characteristics such as spending habits, product preferences, or demographic features.

Step 1: Load the Data

Assume we have a dataset of customer data with features like **annual income**, **spending score**, and **age**.

python

```
import pandas as pd

# Load the customer data
df = pd.read_csv('customer_data.csv')

# Preview the dataset
print(df.head())
```

Step 2: Preprocess the Data

We will extract the relevant features and scale them for clustering algorithms.

python

```
from sklearn.preprocessing import StandardScaler

# Select features
X = df[['Annual Income', 'Spending Score']]

# Standardize the features
scaler = StandardScaler()
X_scaled = scaler.fit_transform(X)
```

Step 3: Apply K-means Clustering

We will use the **K-means clustering algorithm** to group the customers into clusters.

```python
from sklearn.cluster import KMeans

# Apply K-means with 3 clusters
kmeans = KMeans(n_clusters=3)
kmeans.fit(X_scaled)

# Get the cluster labels
labels = kmeans.labels_

# Add the cluster labels to the dataset
df['Cluster'] = labels
```

Step 4: Visualize the Clusters

We will visualize the clusters to understand the segmentation.

```python
import matplotlib.pyplot as plt

# Plot the clusters
plt.scatter(df['Annual  Income'],  df['Spending
Score'], c=df['Cluster'], cmap='viridis')
```

```
plt.xlabel('Annual Income')
plt.ylabel('Spending Score')
plt.title('Customer Segmentation')
plt.show()
```

Step 5: Interpret the Results

By visualizing the clusters, we can identify different customer segments. For example:

- Cluster 1 might consist of high-income, low-spending customers.
- Cluster 2 might consist of low-income, high-spending customers.
- Cluster 3 might be a middle-income group with moderate spending.

Key Takeaways

- **Unsupervised learning** is a type of machine learning where the model learns patterns from data without labeled outputs. The primary tasks are **clustering** and **dimensionality reduction**.
- **Clustering algorithms** like **K-means**, **Hierarchical Clustering**, and **DBSCAN** are used to group similar data points together.

- **PCA (Principal Component Analysis)** is a dimensionality reduction technique that reduces the number of features while preserving the essential information.
- In the **case study**, we performed **customer segmentation** using clustering algorithms and visualized the results to identify distinct customer segments for targeted marketing.

In the next chapter, we will explore **model evaluation techniques** and how to improve the performance of unsupervised learning models.

CHAPTER 12

INTRODUCTION TO DEEP LEARNING

In this chapter, we will introduce you to the exciting world of **Deep Learning**, a subfield of machine learning that focuses on algorithms inspired by the structure and function of the human brain. Deep learning has revolutionized fields such as computer vision, natural language processing, and robotics. We will cover the basics of **neural networks**, the building blocks of deep learning, and explore how deep learning models are different from traditional machine learning models. Additionally, we will introduce popular deep learning frameworks like **TensorFlow** and **Keras** and explore real-world applications where deep learning is used.

What is Deep Learning?

Deep learning is a subset of machine learning that uses **artificial neural networks** with many layers (hence the term "deep") to learn from vast amounts of data. These neural networks consist of multiple layers of nodes (also called **neurons**) that process and transform input data to make predictions or decisions.

144

Deep learning has become increasingly popular due to its ability to learn complex patterns from large datasets. It is particularly effective in tasks like image classification, speech recognition, and natural language processing.

Deep learning models are generally more powerful than traditional machine learning models because they can learn **features** directly from raw data (e.g., pixels in images, words in text), without requiring manual feature engineering.

Neural Networks and the Basics of Perceptrons

At the heart of deep learning lies the concept of **neural networks**, which are computational models inspired by the brain's architecture. The simplest form of a neural network is the **perceptron**, which consists of a single layer of neurons. However, modern deep learning networks are much more complex, consisting of multiple layers of neurons, which allow them to learn more intricate patterns.

1. What is a Perceptron?

A **perceptron** is the most basic type of artificial neuron. It takes several inputs, performs a weighted sum, and passes the result through an activation function to produce an output.

The perceptron has three main components:

1. **Inputs (x)**: These are the features or data points that the perceptron will use to make a decision.
2. **Weights (w)**: Each input is assigned a weight, which represents the importance of that input.
3. **Activation function**: The weighted sum of the inputs is passed through an activation function, which determines whether the perceptron fires (i.e., whether it activates and produces an output).

The output of the perceptron is calculated as:

$y = \sigma\left(\sum_{i} w_i x_i + b \right)$y=σ(i∑ wixi+b)

Where:

- x_ix_ixi is the input feature.
- w_iw_iwi is the weight for the input.
- $b$bb is the bias term.
- σ\sigmaσ is the activation function (often the **step function** for a perceptron).

2. Multilayer Neural Networks

In modern deep learning, neural networks consist of multiple layers of perceptrons, and these layers are divided into:

1. **Input layer**: This layer accepts the raw data.

146

2. **Hidden layers**: These layers perform the transformations and computations. The more hidden layers there are, the deeper the network, which allows it to learn more complex patterns.

3. **Output layer**: This layer produces the final output of the network, such as a classification label or a regression value.

Each layer's output becomes the input for the next layer. This allows neural networks to learn hierarchical representations of data, such as recognizing edges, shapes, and objects in images.

Introduction to TensorFlow and Keras

1. TensorFlow

TensorFlow is an open-source framework developed by Google for building and deploying deep learning models. It provides a comprehensive set of tools, libraries, and community resources to help developers and researchers build sophisticated machine learning and deep learning models.

TensorFlow allows for the creation of **neural networks**, **optimization algorithms**, and **automatic differentiation** (which is essential for training deep learning models via backpropagation). It supports both CPU and GPU computation, making it highly efficient for large-scale deep learning tasks.

Key Features of TensorFlow:

- Scalable and efficient for both training and deployment.
- Supports deep learning tasks like image classification, object detection, and text generation.
- Works well with other tools like **Keras** for model building and **TensorFlow Lite** for mobile devices.

2. Keras

Keras is a high-level neural networks API, written in Python, that runs on top of TensorFlow. It is designed to make building and training deep learning models easier and more intuitive. Keras provides a simplified interface for defining complex neural network architectures, making it accessible to both beginners and experts.

Key Features of Keras:

- Simple and user-friendly interface for building deep learning models.
- Built-in support for neural network layers, optimizers, and loss functions.
- Supports both convolutional networks (CNNs) for image-related tasks and recurrent networks (RNNs) for sequence-based tasks.
- Easily extensible to create custom models and layers.

With Keras, you can define neural networks with just a few lines of code, making it an excellent tool for rapid prototyping.

Example of building a simple neural network with Keras:

```python
import tensorflow as tf
from tensorflow.keras.models import Sequential
from tensorflow.keras.layers import Dense

# Define a simple feedforward neural network
model = Sequential([
    Dense(64,                  activation='relu',
input_shape=(input_dim,)),
    Dense(32, activation='relu'),
    Dense(1, activation='sigmoid')  # For binary
classification
])

# Compile the model
model.compile(optimizer='adam',
loss='binary_crossentropy',
metrics=['accuracy'])

# Train the model
model.fit(X_train,      y_train,      epochs=10,
batch_size=32)
```

```
# Evaluate the model
model.evaluate(X_test, y_test)
```

Difference Between Deep Learning and Machine Learning

Although **deep learning** and **machine learning** are closely related, there are some key differences between them:

- **Machine Learning (ML)**: Machine learning algorithms learn patterns from data and make predictions based on those patterns. In ML, the process of feature extraction is typically done manually, and models like decision trees, support vector machines, and linear regression are commonly used. ML models are often shallow, meaning they consist of a small number of layers or computations.
- **Deep Learning (DL)**: Deep learning is a subset of machine learning that uses **deep neural networks**, which have many layers of neurons. These models automatically learn complex features from raw data, eliminating the need for manual feature engineering. Deep learning is particularly effective for tasks with large amounts of unstructured data, such as images, audio, and text.

Key Differences:

- **Data Requirements**: Deep learning models typically require large amounts of labeled data, whereas machine learning models can work with smaller datasets.

- **Feature Engineering**: In deep learning, feature extraction is learned by the model, while in machine learning, features are typically manually engineered by experts.

- **Model Complexity**: Deep learning models are more complex, with many layers of neurons, while machine learning models tend to be simpler and more interpretable.

- **Performance**: Deep learning often outperforms traditional machine learning algorithms in tasks like image recognition, natural language processing, and speech recognition, especially with large datasets.

Use Cases of Deep Learning in Real-World Applications

Deep learning has had a transformative impact on many industries and has been applied to a wide range of real-world problems. Some key use cases include:

1. Computer Vision

Deep learning, particularly **Convolutional Neural Networks (CNNs)**, has revolutionized computer vision tasks, enabling machines to automatically recognize and classify objects in images and videos. Applications include:

- **Image classification**: Identifying objects or categories in images (e.g., classifying animals, medical images).
- **Object detection**: Locating and classifying objects in images (e.g., autonomous vehicles detecting pedestrians, traffic signs).
- **Facial recognition**: Identifying individuals based on facial features.

2. Natural Language Processing (NLP)

Deep learning has significantly advanced the field of **Natural Language Processing**, where models can understand, generate, and translate human language. Applications include:

- **Sentiment analysis**: Determining the sentiment of a piece of text (e.g., positive, negative, neutral).
- **Machine translation**: Automatically translating text from one language to another (e.g., Google Translate).
- **Speech recognition**: Converting spoken language into text (e.g., voice assistants like Siri and Alexa).

3. Autonomous Vehicles

Deep learning plays a critical role in autonomous driving systems, where neural networks process data from cameras, lidar, and radar sensors to enable a vehicle to navigate and make decisions in real-time. This includes tasks like:

- **Object detection**: Identifying pedestrians, other vehicles, and obstacles.
- **Path planning**: Deciding the best route for the vehicle to take.

4. Healthcare

Deep learning has shown great promise in healthcare applications, such as:

- **Medical image analysis**: Automatically diagnosing diseases from medical images (e.g., detecting tumors in X-rays and MRIs).
- **Drug discovery**: Using deep learning to predict how molecules will interact with each other, accelerating drug development.

5. Gaming and Entertainment

Deep learning is also used to create more realistic AI in video games and movies:

- **Game AI**: Deep learning algorithms can create non-player characters (NPCs) that respond realistically to player actions.

- **Deepfakes**: Deep learning is used to generate realistic images, videos, and audio of people saying or doing things they didn't actually do (though this raises ethical concerns).

Key Takeaways

- **Deep learning** is a subset of machine learning that uses multi-layered neural networks to automatically learn features from raw data, making it highly effective for tasks like image recognition, speech processing, and natural language understanding.
- **Neural networks** are the fundamental building blocks of deep learning. Perceptrons are the simplest form of neural networks, and more complex networks with multiple layers allow the model to learn hierarchical features.
- **TensorFlow** and **Keras** are popular frameworks for building deep learning models, providing tools to easily create and train neural networks.
- Deep learning differs from traditional machine learning in that it automates feature extraction and excels in tasks with large amounts of unstructured data.
- Deep learning is applied in many real-world applications, including **computer vision**, **natural language processing**, **autonomous vehicles**, and **healthcare**.

In the next chapter, we will dive deeper into **advanced neural network architectures**, including **Convolutional Neural Networks (CNNs)** and **Recurrent Neural Networks (RNNs)**, which are specialized for image and sequence data, respectively.

CHAPTER 13

BUILDING YOUR FIRST NEURAL NETWORK

In this chapter, we will guide you through the process of building your first **neural network** using **Keras** and **TensorFlow**, two popular frameworks for deep learning. Neural networks are the foundation of deep learning, and learning how to build and train them is key to understanding how deep learning models work. We will start with the basics, from building a simple neural network to understanding **activation functions** and their role in neural networks. Finally, we will end with a **case study** on **image classification** using a basic neural network.

Introduction to Keras and TensorFlow

TensorFlow is an open-source machine learning framework developed by Google, widely used for building and deploying deep learning models. It supports a variety of machine learning algorithms, including neural networks, and is highly efficient for large-scale tasks.

Keras is a high-level neural networks API that runs on top of TensorFlow (or other backends). It provides a simplified interface for building and training deep learning models, making it much easier to prototype and experiment with different neural network architectures. Keras allows you to define and train models with just a few lines of code.

TensorFlow 2.0 integrated Keras as its official high-level API, making it easier to build deep learning models using the power of TensorFlow with a simplified interface.

To install both frameworks:

```bash

pip install tensorflow
```

Building a Simple Neural Network

In this section, we will build a simple neural network using Keras. We will construct a **feedforward neural network** for a basic task, such as classification. The architecture of a neural network typically consists of:

- **Input layer**: Accepts the raw input data.
- **Hidden layers**: These layers perform transformations on the input data using neurons and activation functions.
- **Output layer**: Produces the final prediction or classification result.

1. Define the Neural Network Architecture

For our simple neural network, we will use the following architecture:

- **Input layer**: Number of neurons equals the number of features in the dataset.
- **Hidden layer**: A layer with several neurons (e.g., 64 neurons).
- **Output layer**: For binary classification, this will have 1 neuron with a **sigmoid** activation function (producing values between 0 and 1).

Here's how to define the neural network using Keras:

python

```
import tensorflow as tf
from tensorflow.keras.models import Sequential
from tensorflow.keras.layers import Dense

# Define the model
model = Sequential()

# Input layer and first hidden layer
model.add(Dense(64,          activation='relu',
input_shape=(X_train.shape[1],)))

# Second hidden layer
```

```
model.add(Dense(32, activation='relu'))

# Output layer (for binary classification)
model.add(Dense(1, activation='sigmoid'))

# Summary of the model architecture
model.summary()
```

- **Sequential**: This class represents a linear stack of layers.
- **Dense**: A fully connected layer where each neuron is connected to all neurons in the previous layer.
- **relu**: The activation function for the hidden layers.
- **sigmoid**: The activation function for the output layer, which is appropriate for binary classification.

2. Compile the Model

Before training the model, you need to **compile** it by specifying the **optimizer**, **loss function**, and **metrics** you want to monitor during training.

- **Optimizer**: Determines how the model's weights are updated based on the loss function. Common optimizers include **Adam**, **SGD**, etc.
- **Loss function**: Measures how well the model is performing. For binary classification, **binary_crossentropy** is typically used.

159

- **Metrics**: These are used to evaluate the performance of the model during training. **Accuracy** is a common metric for classification tasks.

python

```
# Compile the model
model.compile(optimizer='adam',
              loss='binary_crossentropy',
              metrics=['accuracy'])
```

Activation Functions and Their Role in Neural Networks

Activation functions are essential components of neural networks. They determine whether a neuron should be activated or not, based on the weighted sum of inputs. They introduce **non-linearity** into the model, allowing the neural network to learn complex patterns.

Common Activation Functions:

- **ReLU (Rectified Linear Unit)**: This is the most common activation function for hidden layers. It outputs the input directly if it's positive; otherwise, it outputs zero. It helps with the vanishing gradient problem.

$$f(x)=\max(0,x)f(x) = \max(0, x)f(x)=\max(0,x)$$

- **Sigmoid**: The sigmoid function squashes the input into a value between 0 and 1. It is commonly used in the output layer for binary classification problems, as it can be interpreted as a probability.

$$f(x) = \frac{1}{1 + e^{-x}}$$

- **Softmax**: For multi-class classification, softmax normalizes the output of the network to represent a probability distribution over multiple classes.

The activation functions in the hidden layers (ReLU) allow the network to learn complex patterns, while the output layer (Sigmoid) ensures the network's predictions are between 0 and 1, which is suitable for binary classification tasks.

Training and Evaluating the Neural Network

Once the model is defined and compiled, it's time to **train** it on the training data. Training involves using **backpropagation** to adjust the model's weights based on the errors in its predictions.

1. Training the Model

We will train the neural network using the `fit` method. This method requires the training data and labels, as well as the number of epochs (iterations) and batch size (the number of samples used in one forward/backward pass).

python

```
# Train the model
history = model.fit(X_train, y_train, epochs=10,
batch_size=32, validation_data=(X_test, y_test))
```

- **epochs**: The number of times the entire dataset is passed through the network.
- **batch_size**: The number of samples used in one training iteration.
- **validation_data**: Data used to evaluate the model after each epoch.

2. Evaluating the Model

Once the model is trained, we can evaluate its performance on the test set using the `evaluate` method.

python

```
# Evaluate the model on the test data
loss, accuracy = model.evaluate(X_test, y_test)

print(f"Test Loss: {loss}")
print(f"Test Accuracy: {accuracy}")
```

- **Loss**: This represents the error in the model's predictions.
- **Accuracy**: This represents the percentage of correct predictions on the test set.

Case Study: Image Classification with a Basic Neural Network

Let's apply the concepts we've learned by using a **basic neural network** for **image classification**. We'll use the **MNIST dataset**, a well-known dataset of handwritten digits (0-9). This is a simple example of a classification problem, where we'll predict the digit in an image.

Step 1: Load the MNIST Dataset

The MNIST dataset is readily available in **Keras**. It contains 60,000 training images and 10,000 test images of handwritten digits.

python

```python
from tensorflow.keras.datasets import mnist

# Load the MNIST dataset
(X_train, y_train), (X_test, y_test) = mnist.load_data()
```

```
# Normalize the images (convert to float32 and
scale to [0, 1] range)
X_train = X_train.astype('float32') / 255
X_test = X_test.astype('float32') / 255


# Reshape the data to match the input shape of
the neural network
X_train = X_train.reshape((X_train.shape[0], 28,
28, 1))
X_test = X_test.reshape((X_test.shape[0], 28,
28, 1))
```

Step 2: Build the Neural Network Model

We will now define a simple neural network for image classification using the MNIST dataset. The model will have:

- A **flatten layer** to convert the 28x28 pixel image into a 1D array.
- A **fully connected hidden layer**.
- An **output layer** with 10 neurons (one for each digit, 0-9) and **softmax** activation for multi-class classification.

```python
from tensorflow.keras.models import Sequential
from tensorflow.keras.layers import Dense,
Flatten


# Define the model
```

```
model = Sequential([
    Flatten(input_shape=(28, 28, 1)),   # Flatten
the image data
    Dense(128, activation='relu'),       # Hidden
layer
    Dense(10, activation='softmax')      # Output
layer with softmax activation
])

# Compile the model
model.compile(optimizer='adam',
loss='sparse_categorical_crossentropy',
metrics=['accuracy'])
```

Step 3: Train the Model

Now, we will train the model using the training data.

python

```
# Train the model
model.fit(X_train,      y_train,         epochs=5,
batch_size=32)
```

Step 4: Evaluate the Model

Finally, we will evaluate the model's performance on the test set.

python

```
# Evaluate the model on the test data
```

```
loss, accuracy = model.evaluate(X_test, y_test)

print(f"Test Loss: {loss}")
print(f"Test Accuracy: {accuracy}")
```

Key Takeaways

- **Keras** and **TensorFlow** are powerful frameworks for building deep learning models, providing high-level and low-level tools for creating neural networks.
- A **simple neural network** consists of an input layer, one or more hidden layers, and an output layer.
- **Activation functions** like **ReLU** (hidden layers) and **sigmoid/softmax** (output layer) are crucial for introducing non-linearity and enabling the network to learn complex patterns.
- **Training** involves adjusting the network's weights using backpropagation and optimizing the loss function.
- In the **case study**, we demonstrated how to build and train a basic neural network for **image classification** using the MNIST dataset.

In the next chapter, we will explore **Convolutional Neural Networks (CNNs)**, a specialized type of neural network for tasks like image classification, and dive deeper into how these networks are structured and trained for visual tasks.

CHAPTER 14

CONVOLUTIONAL NEURAL NETWORKS (CNNS)

In this chapter, we will explore **Convolutional Neural Networks (CNNs)**, which have revolutionized the field of **image processing** and **computer vision**. CNNs are designed to automatically and adaptively learn spatial hierarchies of features from images, making them ideal for tasks like **image classification**, **object detection**, and **segmentation**. We will cover the **architecture of a CNN**, including convolution layers, pooling layers, and fully connected layers, and demonstrate how to build a CNN for **image classification**. Finally, we will walk through a **case study** of classifying images of **cats and dogs**.

Introduction to CNNs and Their Applications

A **Convolutional Neural Network (CNN)** is a deep learning model designed specifically for analyzing visual data. Unlike traditional fully connected neural networks, CNNs are able to automatically detect patterns like edges, textures, and objects from raw image pixels, making them highly effective for tasks that involve image data.

Some key applications of CNNs include:

- **Image classification**: Identifying the objects in an image (e.g., detecting whether an image contains a cat or a dog).
- **Object detection**: Detecting and localizing multiple objects within an image (e.g., finding cars, pedestrians in an image).
- **Face recognition**: Identifying or verifying faces in images or videos.
- **Medical imaging**: Detecting tumors or abnormalities in X-rays, CT scans, and MRIs.

CNNs have achieved significant success in many of these applications due to their ability to learn hierarchical features directly from images.

Understanding the Architecture of a CNN

CNNs are made up of several types of layers that work together to process image data. Below are the main components of a CNN architecture:

1. Convolution Layers

The **convolution layer** is the core building block of a CNN. It applies **filters (kernels)** to the input image (or the output from previous layers) to extract features such as edges, textures, and patterns. Each filter slides over the input image and performs an element-wise multiplication followed by a summation, producing an output feature map.

The process of applying filters is called **convolution**, which helps in detecting local patterns in the image.

Example of a filter (kernel): A 3x3 filter that detects edges could look like this:

css

```
[-1,  -1,  -1]
[ 0,   0,   0]
[ 1,   1,   1]
```

2. Pooling Layers

After the convolution layer, a **pooling layer** is applied to reduce the spatial dimensions (height and width) of the feature map while retaining the most important information. Pooling helps in reducing the computation cost and making the model invariant to small translations or distortions in the image.

The most common types of pooling are:

- **Max pooling**: Takes the maximum value from a set of values (e.g., from a 2x2 grid of values).
- **Average pooling**: Takes the average of a set of values.

Example: If we apply a 2x2 max pooling operation to the feature map:

```csharp
[1, 2, 3, 4]
[5, 6, 7, 8]
[9, 10, 11, 12]
```

The result after max pooling would be:

```csharp
[6, 8]
[10, 12]
```

3. Fully Connected Layers

After several convolution and pooling layers, the output is passed to one or more **fully connected (dense) layers**. These layers are traditional neural network layers where each neuron is connected to every neuron in the previous layer. The fully connected layers make the final prediction based on the high-level features learned in the earlier layers.

In the case of image classification, the output layer will have as many neurons as there are classes, and a **softmax activation function** is used to output class probabilities.

Building a CNN for Image Classification

Let's walk through building a simple CNN model for **image classification** using **Keras** (with TensorFlow as the backend). For this example, we will classify images of cats and dogs.

Step 1: Import Libraries and Load the Dataset

First, we import necessary libraries and load the dataset. We will use the **Cats vs Dogs dataset**, which contains images of cats and dogs.

python

```python
import tensorflow as tf
from tensorflow.keras.models import Sequential
from tensorflow.keras.layers import Conv2D,
MaxPooling2D, Flatten, Dense, Dropout
from tensorflow.keras.preprocessing.image import
ImageDataGenerator

# Load the Cats vs Dogs dataset
train_dir = 'data/train'
validation_dir = 'data/validation'

# Image preprocessing and augmentation
train_datagen                                      =
ImageDataGenerator(rescale=1./255,
horizontal_flip=True, rotation_range=30)
```

```
validation_datagen                              =
ImageDataGenerator(rescale=1./255)

train_generator                                 =
train_datagen.flow_from_directory(train_dir,
target_size=(150,      150),      batch_size=32,
class_mode='binary')
validation_generator                            =
validation_datagen.flow_from_directory(validati
on_dir,  target_size=(150,  150),  batch_size=32,
class_mode='binary')
```

Here, we use **ImageDataGenerator** to preprocess the images by rescaling them and applying random transformations for augmentation (e.g., rotation and flipping). This helps prevent overfitting.

Step 2: Define the CNN Model

Now, we define the CNN architecture:

```python
# Initialize the CNN
model = Sequential()

# Convolution layer 1
model.add(Conv2D(32, (3, 3), activation='relu',
input_shape=(150, 150, 3)))
```

172

```python
# Max pooling layer 1
model.add(MaxPooling2D(pool_size=(2, 2)))

# Convolution layer 2
model.add(Conv2D(64, (3, 3), activation='relu'))

# Max pooling layer 2
model.add(MaxPooling2D(pool_size=(2, 2)))

# Convolution layer 3
model.add(Conv2D(128,            (3,            3),
activation='relu'))

# Max pooling layer 3
model.add(MaxPooling2D(pool_size=(2, 2)))

# Flatten the output from the convolution layers
model.add(Flatten())

# Fully connected layer
model.add(Dense(128, activation='relu'))
model.add(Dropout(0.5))    # Dropout to prevent
overfitting

# Output layer with softmax activation (binary
classification)
model.add(Dense(1, activation='sigmoid'))
```

```
# Summarize the model architecture
model.summary()
```

This CNN architecture consists of:

- Three convolutional layers (with increasing depth: 32, 64, 128 filters).
- Pooling layers (max pooling with a 2x2 filter) after each convolution.
- A **Flatten** layer to convert the 2D feature maps into a 1D vector.
- A **Dense** fully connected layer with 128 neurons.
- An **Output layer** with a single neuron and **sigmoid activation** for binary classification (cats or dogs).

Step 3: Compile the Model

Now, we compile the model with **binary crossentropy** as the loss function (for binary classification) and the **Adam** optimizer.

```python
python
```

```
# Compile the model
model.compile(optimizer='adam',
loss='binary_crossentropy',
metrics=['accuracy'])
```

Step 4: Train the Model

Now that the model is compiled, we train it using the training and validation data generators.

```python
# Train the model
history = model.fit(train_generator, epochs=10,
validation_data=validation_generator)
```

Step 5: Evaluate the Model

Once training is complete, we can evaluate the model's performance on the test dataset.

```python
# Evaluate the model on the validation data
loss,                  accuracy              =
model.evaluate(validation_generator)
print(f'Validation Loss: {loss}')
print(f'Validation Accuracy: {accuracy}')
```

Case Study: Classifying Images of Cats and Dogs

In this case study, we built a convolutional neural network to classify images of cats and dogs. Here's a recap of the steps we took:

1. **Preprocessed** the images using **ImageDataGenerator** for data augmentation.

2. Defined a **CNN architecture** with convolutional, pooling, and fully connected layers.

3. **Compiled** and trained the model using the **binary crossentropy** loss function.

4. **Evaluated** the model's performance on the validation data.

By training the CNN, the model learns features like edges, shapes, and patterns in the images to distinguish between cats and dogs.

Key Takeaways

- **Convolutional Neural Networks (CNNs)** are specialized neural networks designed for image processing tasks. They excel at learning spatial hierarchies of features from raw image data.
- CNNs typically consist of:
  - **Convolution layers**: To extract features from images.
  - **Pooling layers**: To reduce dimensionality and retain important information.
  - **Fully connected layers**: To make predictions based on the learned features.

- **Keras** and **TensorFlow** provide powerful tools for building, training, and deploying CNNs.
- In the **case study**, we built a CNN for classifying images of cats and dogs, trained it on the dataset, and evaluated its performance.

In the next chapter, we will explore **advanced CNN architectures**, such as **ResNet** and **VGG**, and learn how to fine-tune these models for more complex tasks.

CHAPTER 15

RECURRENT NEURAL NETWORKS (RNNS)

In this chapter, we will explore **Recurrent Neural Networks (RNNs)**, a class of neural networks designed for sequential data. Unlike traditional feedforward neural networks, RNNs are specifically designed to handle sequences of data, such as time series, text, or speech. We will dive into their architecture, applications, and key improvements like **Long Short-Term Memory (LSTM)** networks. We will also explore a **case study** involving **sentiment analysis of tweets** using RNNs.

What Are RNNs and How Do They Differ from Traditional Neural Networks?

Recurrent Neural Networks (RNNs) are a type of neural network designed to process sequences of data. Unlike traditional **feedforward neural networks**, where information moves only in one direction (from input to output), RNNs have **connections that loop back on themselves**, allowing them to maintain a memory of previous inputs in the sequence. This looped architecture gives

178

RNNs the ability to capture temporal dependencies, making them particularly useful for tasks that involve sequential data.

The key feature of RNNs is that they have an internal **state** (memory), which gets updated at each time step as new inputs are provided. This allows RNNs to make predictions based not just on the current input but also on past inputs, enabling them to recognize patterns over time.

Difference Between RNNs and Traditional Neural Networks

- **Feedforward Neural Networks (FNNs)**: In traditional neural networks, the data flows in one direction from input to output. There's no notion of memory, so they're best suited for tasks where input data is independent (e.g., classification of images).
- **Recurrent Neural Networks (RNNs)**: In RNNs, the output of each time step is dependent on the current input as well as the previous output (memory). This makes them suited for sequential data, where the order of data matters (e.g., time series forecasting, speech recognition, or language translation).

179

Applications of RNNs in AI: Time Series, Text, and Speech

RNNs are used in a variety of applications where data is sequential and past information is important for predicting future values or interpreting current input.

1. Time Series Analysis

Time series data consists of observations collected over time (e.g., stock prices, weather data). RNNs can be used to model temporal dependencies and make predictions about future values based on past data. For example:

- **Stock market prediction**: Predicting future stock prices based on historical data.
- **Weather forecasting**: Predicting future weather conditions based on historical temperature and pressure data.

2. Natural Language Processing (NLP)

RNNs are widely used in text-based applications because text is inherently sequential. RNNs process one word or character at a time and remember previous words, which is essential for tasks like:

- **Language modeling**: Predicting the next word in a sentence.

- **Machine translation**: Translating text from one language to another.
- **Speech recognition**: Converting spoken words into text.

3. Speech Recognition

Speech recognition is another area where RNNs are highly effective. Given the temporal nature of speech, RNNs are able to capture the dependencies between the different phonemes, words, and sentences. This is used in applications like:

- **Voice assistants**: Siri, Google Assistant, and Alexa rely on speech recognition powered by RNNs to understand and respond to user queries.
- **Transcribing audio**: Converting speech to text, especially in noisy environments.

Introduction to Long Short-Term Memory (LSTM) Networks

While RNNs are powerful for sequential data, they suffer from one significant problem: the **vanishing gradient problem**. During training, the gradients used to update the weights of the network can become very small, making it difficult for the network to learn long-term dependencies. This is especially problematic when the sequences are long.

Long Short-Term Memory (LSTM) networks are a type of RNN specifically designed to address this problem. LSTMs use **gates** to control the flow of information through the network, allowing them to maintain long-term dependencies.

LSTM Components:

1. **Forget gate**: Decides which information from the previous cell state should be discarded.
2. **Input gate**: Updates the cell state with new information from the current input.
3. **Output gate**: Decides the next hidden state based on the current cell state and input.

By regulating what information is remembered and forgotten, LSTMs can retain important long-term dependencies, making them much more effective than standard RNNs for tasks that require understanding long sequences.

Example of defining an LSTM layer in Keras:

python

```
from tensorflow.keras.models import Sequential
from tensorflow.keras.layers import LSTM, Dense

# Define a simple LSTM model
model = Sequential()
```

```
# Add an LSTM layer with 50 units and return
sequences to feed the next layer
model.add(LSTM(50,        return_sequences=True,
input_shape=(X_train.shape[1], 1)))

# Add a fully connected layer for prediction
model.add(Dense(1))

# Compile the model
model.compile(optimizer='adam',
loss='mean_squared_error')
```

Case Study: Sentiment Analysis of Tweets Using RNNs

In this case study, we will use an **RNN (or LSTM)** to perform **sentiment analysis** on a dataset of **tweets**. The task is to classify the sentiment of each tweet as either positive or negative.

Step 1: Load the Dataset

For simplicity, let's assume we have a dataset with tweets and their associated sentiment labels (1 for positive sentiment and 0 for negative sentiment). We will use the **Twitter Sentiment Analysis dataset** or a similar dataset.

python

```
import pandas as pd

# Load the tweet data
df = pd.read_csv('tweets.csv')

# Preview the data
print(df.head())
```

The dataset contains two columns:

- **Text**: The tweet text.
- **Label**: The sentiment label (1 for positive, 0 for negative).

Step 2: Preprocess the Text Data

Before feeding the text data into an RNN, we need to preprocess it. This typically involves:

1. **Tokenization**: Converting text into a sequence of words or tokens.
2. **Padding**: Ensuring all sequences have the same length.

```python
from tensorflow.keras.preprocessing.text import Tokenizer
from tensorflow.keras.preprocessing.sequence import pad_sequences
```

```
# Initialize the tokenizer
tokenizer = Tokenizer(num_words=10000)

# Tokenize the tweet texts
tokenizer.fit_on_texts(df['Text'])
X = tokenizer.texts_to_sequences(df['Text'])

# Pad the sequences to ensure they all have the
same length
X_pad    =    pad_sequences(X,    padding='post',
maxlen=100)

# Labels
y = df['Label']
```

Step 3: Define the RNN/LSTM Model

Now, we will define an RNN model (or LSTM model) to perform the sentiment classification.

```
python
```

```
from tensorflow.keras.models import Sequential
from tensorflow.keras.layers import Embedding,
LSTM, Dense

# Define the model
model = Sequential()
```

```
# Add an embedding layer (word embeddings to
convert words into vectors)
model.add(Embedding(input_dim=10000,
output_dim=128, input_length=100))


# Add an LSTM layer
model.add(LSTM(128, return_sequences=False))


# Add a fully connected layer for classification
model.add(Dense(1, activation='sigmoid'))


# Compile the model
model.compile(optimizer='adam',
loss='binary_crossentropy',
metrics=['accuracy'])
```

Step 4: Train the Model

Now, we train the model on the preprocessed data.

```
python
```

```
# Train the model
model.fit(X_pad, y, epochs=5, batch_size=64,
validation_split=0.2)
```

Step 5: Evaluate the Model

Finally, we evaluate the performance of the trained model.

```
python
```

```
# Evaluate the model
loss, accuracy = model.evaluate(X_pad, y)


print(f"Test Loss: {loss}")
print(f"Test Accuracy: {accuracy}")
```

Key Takeaways

- **Recurrent Neural Networks (RNNs)** are designed for processing sequential data and are widely used in tasks such as time series analysis, speech recognition, and natural language processing (NLP).
- **Long Short-Term Memory (LSTM)** networks are a type of RNN that solves the vanishing gradient problem, enabling the network to retain long-term dependencies.
- **Applications of RNNs** include time series forecasting, text classification, speech recognition, and language modeling.
- In the **case study**, we used an **LSTM model** to perform sentiment analysis on tweets, classifying them as positive or negative.
- **Text preprocessing** steps like tokenization and padding are essential for preparing data for RNNs.

In the next chapter, we will dive deeper into **advanced topics in RNNs** such as **Bidirectional RNNs**, **Attention Mechanisms**, and

Transformers, which are designed to handle more complex sequence-based tasks.

CHAPTER 16

NATURAL LANGUAGE PROCESSING (NLP)

In this chapter, we will introduce you to **Natural Language Processing (NLP)**, a branch of artificial intelligence that focuses on enabling computers to understand, interpret, and generate human language. We will cover the essential NLP techniques, including basic text processing methods such as **tokenization**, **stemming**, and **lemmatization**, and explore how these can be used in **text classification** tasks. Additionally, we will delve into the use of **deep learning** for NLP, particularly focusing on **word embeddings** like **Word2Vec** and **GloVe**. Finally, we will walk through a **case study** where we build a simple **chatbot** using NLP techniques.

Introduction to NLP and Its Applications

Natural Language Processing (NLP) is a field of AI focused on enabling machines to interact with human language in a meaningful way. NLP bridges the gap between human communication and computer understanding by converting human language into a format that machines can process.

Some common applications of NLP include:

- **Text classification**: Assigning labels or categories to text, such as sentiment analysis or spam detection.
- **Machine translation**: Translating text from one language to another (e.g., Google Translate).
- **Speech recognition**: Converting spoken language into written text (e.g., voice assistants like Siri and Alexa).
- **Named Entity Recognition (NER)**: Identifying entities like names, dates, and locations within text.
- **Chatbots and virtual assistants**: Engaging in conversations with users and providing responses to their queries.

NLP is widely used in applications ranging from customer service chatbots to automated content generation and sentiment analysis of social media posts.

Basic Text Processing Techniques: Tokenization, Stemming, and Lemmatization

Before applying machine learning or deep learning algorithms to text data, it's crucial to preprocess the text. Below are some basic text processing techniques:

1. Tokenization

Tokenization is the process of breaking down text into smaller units, typically words or sentences. This is the first step in most NLP tasks. After tokenization, the text can be processed at a word level, sentence level, or even at the character level.

- **Word Tokenization**: Splitting text into individual words.
- **Sentence Tokenization**: Splitting text into individual sentences.

Example:

```python
from nltk.tokenize import word_tokenize, sent_tokenize

text = "Hello, world! How are you?"

# Word tokenization
words = word_tokenize(text)
print(words)

# Sentence tokenization
sentences = sent_tokenize(text)
print(sentences)
```

2. Stemming

Stemming is the process of reducing words to their base or root form. For example, "running" becomes "run", and "happily" becomes "happi". Stemming algorithms, such as **Porter Stemmer**, are typically used to reduce words to their base form for further processing.

- Example: "running" → "run", "better" → "better"

Example:

python

```
from nltk.stem import PorterStemmer

stemmer = PorterStemmer()
word = "running"
stemmed_word = stemmer.stem(word)
print(stemmed_word)
```

3. Lemmatization

Lemmatization is a more advanced technique than stemming. Instead of simply chopping off suffixes, lemmatization involves converting a word into its correct base form (or lemma) based on its meaning and context. For instance, "better" becomes "good", and "running" becomes "run".

Lemmatization requires knowledge of the word's part of speech (POS), so it's typically more accurate than stemming.

- Example: "better" → "good", "running" → "run"

Example:

```python
from nltk.stem import WordNetLemmatizer

lemmatizer = WordNetLemmatizer()
word = "running"
lemma = lemmatizer.lemmatize(word, pos='v')    # 'v' for verb
print(lemma)
```

Text Classification with Machine Learning

Text classification is one of the fundamental tasks in NLP, where we assign predefined labels to text data. This can be applied to tasks such as **spam detection**, **sentiment analysis**, and **topic classification**.

1. Preprocessing Text for Classification

Before feeding text into a machine learning model, we need to convert it into a numerical format. Common preprocessing steps include:

- **Removing stop words**: Common words like "the", "and", "is", which don't contribute much to the meaning of the text.
- **Vectorization**: Converting text into numerical features using techniques like **TF-IDF** or **word embeddings**.

2. TF-IDF Vectorization

TF-IDF (Term Frequency - Inverse Document Frequency) is a statistical measure used to evaluate the importance of a word in a document relative to a corpus of documents. It's widely used for converting text data into numerical features.

Example in Python:

```python
python

from sklearn.feature_extraction.text import TfidfVectorizer

# Sample documents
documents = ["I love programming", "Python is great for AI", "I love AI and programming"]
```

```
# TF-IDF vectorization
vectorizer = TfidfVectorizer()
X = vectorizer.fit_transform(documents)


print(X.toarray())
```

3. Classification Model

Once the text is vectorized, we can train a **classification model** using algorithms like **Logistic Regression**, **Naive Bayes**, or **Support Vector Machines (SVM)**.

Example of training a classifier:

```
python


from sklearn.naive_bayes import MultinomialNB
from        sklearn.model_selection        import
train_test_split


#   Labels   (e.g.,   '0'   for   negative,   '1'   for
positive sentiment)
labels = [1, 1, 1]  # Positive sentiment for all
sample texts


# Train-test split
X_train,    X_test,    y_train,    y_test    =
train_test_split(X,    labels,    test_size=0.33,
random_state=42)
```

```
# Train a Naive Bayes classifier
classifier = MultinomialNB()
classifier.fit(X_train, y_train)

# Predict on test data
predictions = classifier.predict(X_test)
print(predictions)
```

Using Deep Learning for NLP: Word Embeddings (Word2Vec, GloVe)

Word embeddings are a form of word representation that allows words with similar meanings to have a similar representation. Word embeddings are crucial for deep learning-based NLP models.

1. Word2Vec

Word2Vec is a popular technique for learning word embeddings, where words are mapped to vectors in a continuous vector space. Word2Vec uses two primary models:

- **Skip-gram model**: Predicts surrounding words based on a given word.
- **Continuous Bag of Words (CBOW)**: Predicts a word based on the surrounding words.

Word2Vec can be trained on a large corpus of text to produce word embeddings, which can then be used in downstream NLP tasks.

2. GloVe (Global Vectors for Word Representation)

GloVe is another algorithm for learning word embeddings, but it differs from Word2Vec in its approach. GloVe uses matrix factorization techniques on the word co-occurrence matrix to generate word vectors that capture the global statistical information of the corpus.

Case Study: Building a Chatbot with NLP Techniques

In this case study, we will build a simple **chatbot** using NLP techniques. Our chatbot will respond to user queries based on predefined responses.

Step 1: Preprocessing the Data

Let's assume we have a small dataset of questions and answers for our chatbot. We will preprocess the text using tokenization, lemmatization, and vectorization (TF-IDF).

```python
import numpy as np
```

```
from    sklearn.feature_extraction.text    import
TfidfVectorizer
from         sklearn.metrics.pairwise        import
cosine_similarity

# Sample data
questions  =  ["How  are  you?",  "What  is  your
name?", "What do you do?"]
answers  =  ["I'm  fine,  thank  you!",  "I  am  a
chatbot.", "I am here to assist you."]

# Preprocessing: Tokenization and lemmatization
would typically go here (simplified for now)
vectorizer = TfidfVectorizer()
X = vectorizer.fit_transform(questions)
```

Step 2: Building the Response Function

Now, we'll define a function that takes the user's input, computes the cosine similarity with the existing questions, and returns the most appropriate answer.

```
python
```

```
def chatbot_response(user_input):
    # Preprocess the user input
    user_input_vec                            =
vectorizer.transform([user_input])
```

```
    # Compute the cosine similarity between the
user input and the preprocessed questions
    similarity                              =
cosine_similarity(user_input_vec, X)


    # Get the index of the highest similarity
score
    best_match_idx = np.argmax(similarity)


    # Return the corresponding answer
    return answers[best_match_idx]

# Test the chatbot
user_input = "What is your name?"
response = chatbot_response(user_input)
print(f"Chatbot: {response}")
```

Step 3: Improving the Chatbot

To improve the chatbot, you can integrate more advanced NLP techniques, such as:

- **Named Entity Recognition (NER)** for extracting entities like dates or locations.
- **Sequence-to-sequence models** for handling more complex conversations.

199

Key Takeaways

- **Natural Language Processing (NLP)** is a field of AI focused on enabling machines to understand and interact with human language.

- Basic text processing techniques, such as **tokenization, stemming**, and **lemmatization**, are essential for cleaning and preparing text data for machine learning models.

- **Text classification** involves transforming text into numerical features (using TF-IDF) and applying machine learning models for tasks like sentiment analysis and spam detection.

- **Word embeddings** like **Word2Vec** and **GloVe** are crucial for representing words as dense vectors that capture their semantic meaning.

- In the **case study**, we built a simple chatbot that responds to user queries by calculating the cosine similarity between the input and predefined questions.

In the next chapter, we will explore **advanced NLP models** like **Transformers**, **BERT**, and **GPT**, which have pushed the boundaries of NLP tasks and achieved state-of-the-art performance in tasks like language generation and understanding.

CHAPTER 17

REINFORCEMENT LEARNING

In this chapter, we will explore **Reinforcement Learning (RL)**, an area of machine learning where an agent learns how to make decisions by interacting with its environment. Unlike supervised learning, where the model is trained on labeled data, reinforcement learning involves learning from feedback in the form of rewards or penalties. We will discuss the key components of RL, introduce fundamental algorithms like **Q-learning** and **policy gradients**, and explore real-world applications. Finally, we will walk through a **case study** on building a simple RL model.

What is Reinforcement Learning?

Reinforcement Learning (RL) is a type of machine learning where an **agent** learns to make decisions by performing actions in an **environment** and receiving feedback through **rewards** or **punishments**. The goal of RL is to train the agent to maximize its cumulative reward over time by learning the best actions to take in different states of the environment.

Key characteristics of RL:

- The agent **interacts** with its environment.

201

- The environment responds to the agent's actions and provides feedback (rewards or penalties).

- The agent aims to **maximize cumulative rewards** over time (not necessarily immediate rewards).

RL is typically used for problems where the correct output is not known in advance, and the agent must learn from experience.

Key Components of Reinforcement Learning: Agent, Environment, Reward System

The core components of an RL system are:

1. Agent

The **agent** is the decision-maker. It interacts with the environment, observes its state, and takes actions based on the current state. The goal of the agent is to learn the best strategy to maximize cumulative rewards.

2. Environment

The **environment** is everything the agent interacts with. It can be a physical system (e.g., a robot navigating a room) or a virtual system (e.g., a game). The environment receives the actions from the agent and returns the resulting state and a reward.

3. Reward System

The **reward system** provides feedback to the agent based on its actions. After taking an action, the agent receives a reward (positive or negative) based on how well it performed the task. The agent's objective is to maximize the total accumulated reward over time.

The feedback is typically represented as:

- **Immediate reward**: The reward received after taking a specific action.
- **Cumulative reward**: The total reward over time, which the agent aims to maximize.

4. States and Actions

- **State (s)**: The current situation or configuration of the environment. It provides all the information the agent needs to make a decision.
- **Action (a)**: The decision made by the agent to transition from one state to another. The set of all possible actions is called the **action space**.

An RL task involves the agent learning the optimal policy (a mapping from states to actions) to maximize the long-term reward.

Introduction to Q-learning and Policy Gradients

There are several algorithms in RL, and two of the most popular ones are **Q-learning** and **Policy Gradients**.

1. Q-learning

Q-learning is a model-free RL algorithm where the agent learns the value of taking a particular action in a particular state. The value is represented by a **Q-table** (or **Q-function**), where each entry $Q(s,a)Q(s, a)Q(s,a)$ stores the expected future rewards for taking action aaa in state sss.

The goal of Q-learning is to learn the **optimal Q-values**, which allow the agent to select the best action in each state. The agent updates the Q-values iteratively using the **Bellman equation**:

$Q(s,a) \leftarrow Q(s,a) + \alpha(r + \gamma \max_{a'} Q(s',a') - Q(s,a))Q(s, a)$ \leftarrow $Q(s, a) + $ \alpha \left($r + $ \gamma \max_{a'\} $Q(s', a') - Q(s, a)$ \right)$Q(s,a) \leftarrow Q(s,a) + \alpha(r + \gamma a' \max Q(s',a') - Q(s,a))$

Where:

- α\alpha$\alpha$ is the learning rate.
- rrr is the reward received after taking action aaa in state sss.

- γ\gamma$\gamma$ is the discount factor (how much future rewards are valued compared to immediate rewards).
- $\max_{a'} Q(s',a')$\max_{a'} Q(s', a')$\max a'Q(s',a')$ is the maximum expected future reward from the next state $s'$$s'$$s'$.

2. Policy Gradients

Policy gradients is another RL algorithm, but instead of learning Q-values, it directly learns the **policy** (a probability distribution over actions). Policy gradient methods aim to maximize the expected cumulative reward by adjusting the policy based on the feedback from the environment.

- **Policy**: A function that maps states to actions. In the case of continuous actions, the policy is usually a probability distribution.
- **Objective**: The objective is to maximize the expected reward by adjusting the policy parameters, often using techniques like **stochastic gradient ascent**.

Policy gradient methods are particularly useful in environments with large or continuous action spaces, where Q-learning may not be as effective.

Real-World Applications: Gaming, Robotics

Reinforcement learning has found applications in a wide range of fields. Below are a few examples of where RL is commonly applied:

1. Gaming

One of the most famous RL applications is in video game playing. **AlphaGo**, developed by DeepMind, used RL to defeat the world champion in the game of **Go**. In gaming, RL agents can learn to play games by interacting with the game environment, receiving rewards based on game performance, and improving through trial and error.

- **Game-playing AI**: RL is used in developing AI agents that can learn to play video games like chess, Go, and Dota 2 at superhuman levels.

2. Robotics

RL is also widely used in robotics, where robots learn to perform tasks through trial and error. The robots are trained to complete tasks such as object manipulation, navigation, and control.

- **Robotic control**: Teaching a robot to walk, grasp objects, or move efficiently through an environment.

- **Autonomous vehicles**: Self-driving cars use RL to make decisions about navigation and obstacle avoidance.

Case Study: Building a Simple Reinforcement Learning Model

Let's walk through a simple RL case study where we build an agent to navigate a grid environment. The task of the agent is to reach the goal (represented as a specific cell) while avoiding obstacles.

Step 1: Define the Environment

Let's define a simple grid where:

- **S** represents the starting point.
- **G** represents the goal.
- **O** represents obstacles.
- **.** represents empty spaces.

```mathematica
S . . . .
. O . O .
. . . . G
```

Step 2: Implement the Q-learning Algorithm

Here's a basic implementation of Q-learning for this environment. The agent will learn to navigate the grid using Q-values.

```python
import numpy as np
import random

# Define the grid environment
grid_size = (3, 5)
goal = (2, 4)
obstacles = [(1, 1), (1, 3)]

# Define the actions: up, down, left, right
actions = ['up', 'down', 'left', 'right']

# Initialize Q-table (state, action)
Q = np.zeros((grid_size[0], grid_size[1], len(actions)))

# Hyperparameters
alpha = 0.1   # Learning rate
gamma = 0.9   # Discount factor
epsilon = 0.2   # Exploration rate

# Function to get the possible actions for a given state
```

```python
def get_possible_actions(state):
    x, y = state
    possible_actions = []
    if x > 0: possible_actions.append('up')
    if x < grid_size[0] - 1:
possible_actions.append('down')
    if y > 0: possible_actions.append('left')
    if y < grid_size[1] - 1:
possible_actions.append('right')
    return possible_actions


# Reward function
def get_reward(state):
    if state == goal:
        return 1  # Goal reached
    elif state in obstacles:
        return -1  # Hit an obstacle
    else:
        return 0  # Regular move


# Q-learning algorithm
def q_learning(episodes):
    for episode in range(episodes):
        state = (0, 0)  # Start from top-left
corner
        done = False
        while not done:
            if random.uniform(0, 1) < epsilon:
```

```
            action                        =
random.choice(get_possible_actions(state))     #
Exploration
            else:
                # Exploitation: Choose the best
action based on Q-values
                action                        =
actions[np.argmax(Q[state[0], state[1]])]


            # Take action and observe next state
            if action == 'up':
                next_state = (state[0] - 1,
state[1])
            elif action == 'down':
                next_state = (state[0] + 1,
state[1])
            elif action == 'left':
                next_state = (state[0], state[1]
- 1)
            elif action == 'right':
                next_state = (state[0], state[1]
+ 1)


            # Update Q-table using the Bellman
equation
            reward = get_reward(next_state)
            Q[state[0],                state[1],
actions.index(action)] += alpha * (
```

```
                reward        +        gamma        *
np.max(Q[next_state[0],      next_state[1]])        -
Q[state[0], state[1], actions.index(action)]
            )

        state = next_state

        # Terminate if goal is reached
        if state == goal:
            done = True

# Run Q-learning for 1000 episodes
q_learning(1000)

# Print the learned Q-table
print(Q)
```

Step 3: Evaluate the Model

After training, we can evaluate the learned Q-table by checking which action leads to the goal with the highest Q-value for each state.

Key Takeaways

- **Reinforcement Learning (RL)** enables agents to learn through trial and error by interacting with an environment and receiving feedback (rewards or penalties).

- The key components of RL include the **agent**, **environment**, and **reward system**.
- **Q-learning** and **policy gradients** are two popular RL algorithms. Q-learning focuses on learning Q-values, while policy gradients directly optimize the policy.
- RL has a wide range of applications, including **gaming**, **robotics**, and **autonomous vehicles**.
- In the **case study**, we built a simple Q-learning agent to navigate a grid environment and reach a goal while avoiding obstacles.

In the next chapter, we will explore **advanced RL techniques**, such as **Deep Q-Learning** and **Actor-Critic Methods**, to handle more complex environments.

CHAPTER 18

MODEL EVALUATION AND HYPERPARAMETER TUNING

In this chapter, we will discuss essential concepts in **model evaluation** and **hyperparameter tuning** that are crucial for building high-performing machine learning models. We will explore techniques to assess the performance of your models, such as detecting **overfitting** and **underfitting**, using **cross-validation** for reliable evaluation, and employing **hyperparameter tuning** techniques like **GridSearchCV** and **RandomizedSearchCV** to find the best model configuration. Additionally, we will cover **regularization** methods (L1 and L2) that help prevent overfitting. We will conclude with a **case study** focused on **optimizing a classification model**.

Understanding Overfitting and Underfitting

Before evaluating models, it's essential to understand the concepts of **overfitting** and **underfitting**, as these issues can significantly impact the performance of your model.

213

1. Overfitting

Overfitting occurs when a model learns the **training data** too well, capturing not only the underlying patterns but also the noise and anomalies specific to the training set. As a result, the model performs exceptionally well on the training data but poorly on **new, unseen data** (test data). This means that the model generalizes poorly to new data.

- **Signs of Overfitting**:
    - High accuracy on the training set and low accuracy on the test set.
    - The model is too complex for the task (e.g., too many parameters or deep layers).

2. Underfitting

Underfitting happens when a model is too simple to capture the underlying patterns in the data. It results in poor performance on both the training and test sets because the model is unable to learn the structure of the data properly.

- **Signs of Underfitting**:
    - Low accuracy on both the training and test sets.
    - The model is too simple (e.g., a linear model for a non-linear problem).

Balance Between Overfitting and Underfitting

To build a robust model, the goal is to find the **right balance** between overfitting and underfitting. This means choosing the right model complexity, which is neither too simple nor too complex for the data at hand.

Cross-Validation Techniques for Model Evaluation

Cross-validation is a technique used to evaluate the performance of a model by splitting the dataset into multiple subsets (folds). The model is trained on some of the folds and evaluated on the remaining fold(s), and this process is repeated multiple times to ensure the model's performance is consistent across different subsets of the data.

1. K-Fold Cross-Validation

In **K-fold cross-validation**, the dataset is split into **K** equally sized folds. The model is trained on **K-1** folds and tested on the remaining fold. This process is repeated **K** times, and the performance metrics are averaged to give a more reliable estimate of the model's performance.

- **Steps**:
    1. Split the data into **K** folds.

2. Train the model on **K-1** folds and test it on the remaining fold.

3. Repeat the process **K** times (each time using a different fold for testing).

4. Calculate the average performance across all folds.

- **Example**:

python

```
from        sklearn.model_selection        import
cross_val_score
from          sklearn.ensemble          import
RandomForestClassifier

# Define the model
model = RandomForestClassifier()

# Perform 5-fold cross-validation
scores = cross_val_score(model, X, y, cv=5)

print(f"Cross-validation scores: {scores}")
print(f"Average score: {scores.mean()}")
```

2. Stratified K-Fold Cross-Validation

In **Stratified K-Fold Cross-Validation**, each fold preserves the percentage of samples for each class (particularly useful for imbalanced datasets). This ensures that each fold is representative of the overall distribution of the target variable.

```python

from        sklearn.model_selection        import
StratifiedKFold
from        sklearn.model_selection        import
cross_val_score

# Define the model
model = RandomForestClassifier()

# Stratified K-Fold with 5 splits
skf = StratifiedKFold(n_splits=5)

# Perform cross-validation
scores = cross_val_score(model, X, y, cv=skf)

print(f"Cross-validation scores: {scores}")
print(f"Average score: {scores.mean()}")
```

Hyperparameter   Tuning   Using   GridSearchCV   and RandomizedSearchCV

Hyperparameter tuning involves selecting the optimal values for a model's hyperparameters (parameters that are not learned during training, such as the learning rate, the number of trees in a random forest, or the depth of a decision tree). Proper hyperparameter tuning is crucial for improving the model's performance.

1. GridSearchCV

GridSearchCV is an exhaustive search method that tests all possible combinations of a set of hyperparameters. It trains the model for every combination and evaluates its performance, returning the set of hyperparameters that yields the best performance.

- **Example**:

python

```
from sklearn.model_selection import GridSearchCV
from          sklearn.ensemble          import
RandomForestClassifier

# Define the model
model = RandomForestClassifier()

# Define the hyperparameters to tune
param_grid = {'n_estimators': [50, 100, 200],
'max_depth': [5, 10, 15]}

# Perform GridSearchCV with 5-fold cross-
validation
```

```
grid_search = GridSearchCV(model, param_grid,
cv=5)
grid_search.fit(X_train, y_train)

# Best hyperparameters
print(f"Best                    parameters:
{grid_search.best_params_}")
```

2. RandomizedSearchCV

RandomizedSearchCV performs a random search over the hyperparameter space, testing a fixed number of random combinations. This is less computationally expensive than GridSearchCV and can be more effective when the hyperparameter space is large.

- **Example**:

```
python

from        sklearn.model_selection        import
RandomizedSearchCV
from          sklearn.ensemble          import
RandomForestClassifier
import numpy as np

# Define the model
model = RandomForestClassifier()

# Define the hyperparameters to tune
```

```
param_dist = {'n_estimators': np.arange(50, 200,
50), 'max_depth': [5, 10, 15, 20]}

# Perform RandomizedSearchCV with 5-fold cross-
validation
random_search    =    RandomizedSearchCV(model,
param_dist, n_iter=10, cv=5)
random_search.fit(X_train, y_train)

# Best hyperparameters
print(f"Best                    parameters:
{random_search.best_params_}")
```

Regularization Techniques: L1, L2

Regularization techniques are used to prevent overfitting by penalizing large coefficients in the model. Two common types of regularization are **L1 regularization (Lasso)** and **L2 regularization (Ridge)**.

1. L1 Regularization (Lasso)

L1 regularization adds the absolute value of the coefficients to the loss function. This can lead to sparse models where some feature weights are driven to zero, effectively performing feature selection.

- **Formula**:

Loss=Lossoriginal+λ∑i|wi|\text{Loss} = \text{Loss}_{\text{original}} + \lambda \sum_{i} |w_i|Loss=Lossoriginal+λi∑|wi|

Where λ\lambdaλ is the regularization parameter.

2. L2 Regularization (Ridge)

L2 regularization adds the squared value of the coefficients to the loss function. This prevents the model from assigning excessively large weights to any feature but doesn't lead to sparse models.

- **Formula**:

Loss=Lossoriginal+λ∑iwi2\text{Loss} = \text{Loss}_{\text{original}} + \lambda \sum_{i} w_i^2Loss=Lossoriginal+λi∑wi2

Example of using L1 and L2 regularization in logistic regression:

```python
from        sklearn.linear_model        import
LogisticRegression

# L1 regularization (Lasso)
```

```
model_lasso  =  LogisticRegression(penalty='l1',
solver='liblinear')
model_lasso.fit(X_train, y_train)

# L2 regularization (Ridge)
model_ridge = LogisticRegression(penalty='l2')
model_ridge.fit(X_train, y_train)
```

Case Study: Optimizing a Classification Model

Let's consider the task of optimizing a classification model using **GridSearchCV** and **cross-validation**. We will use the **Iris dataset**, a popular dataset for classification tasks, and train a **Random Forest Classifier** to predict the species of flowers.

Step 1: Load the Dataset
python

```
from sklearn.datasets import load_iris
from        sklearn.model_selection         import
train_test_split

# Load the Iris dataset
data = load_iris()
X = data.data
y = data.target

# Split the data into training and test sets
```

```
X_train,      X_test,      y_train,      y_test      =
train_test_split(X,      y,      test_size=0.3,
random_state=42)
```

Step 2: Define the Model and Hyperparameters

python

```python
from            sklearn.ensemble            import
RandomForestClassifier
from sklearn.model_selection import GridSearchCV

# Define the model
model = RandomForestClassifier()

# Define the hyperparameters to tune
param_grid = {
    'n_estimators': [50, 100, 200],
    'max_depth': [10, 20, None],
    'min_samples_split': [2, 5, 10]
}

# Perform GridSearchCV with 5-fold cross-
validation
grid_search = GridSearchCV(model, param_grid,
cv=5)
grid_search.fit(X_train, y_train)

# Get the best hyperparameters
print(f"Best                        parameters:
{grid_search.best_params_}")
```

Step 3: Evaluate the Model

python

```
# Evaluate the best model on the test set
best_model = grid_search.best_estimator_
test_accuracy = best_model.score(X_test, y_test)
print(f"Test accuracy: {test_accuracy}")
```

Key Takeaways

- **Overfitting** and **underfitting** are common challenges in machine learning. The goal is to balance the model's complexity to avoid both extremes.

- **Cross-validation** techniques, such as **K-fold** and **Stratified K-fold**, provide more reliable performance estimates by testing the model on different subsets of data.

- **Hyperparameter tuning** using methods like **GridSearchCV** and **RandomizedSearchCV** helps to find the optimal hyperparameters for your model, improving its performance.

- **Regularization** techniques like **L1** and **L2** prevent overfitting by penalizing large coefficients in the model.

- In the **case study**, we demonstrated how to use **GridSearchCV** to optimize the hyperparameters of a Random Forest model on the Iris dataset and evaluated its performance.

In the next chapter, we will explore **ensemble methods**, such as **Random Forests** and **Gradient Boosting**, which combine multiple models to improve performance and robustness.

CHAPTER 19

MODEL DEPLOYMENT AND SERVING

In this chapter, we will cover the crucial topic of **model deployment**, which involves taking a trained machine learning model and making it available for use in real-world applications. This is a critical step in the machine learning workflow as it allows your model to serve predictions to users or other systems. We will walk through techniques for **saving** and **loading** models, deploying models using **Flask** or **FastAPI** for web services, and using **cloud platforms** like **AWS** and **Google Cloud** for deployment. Lastly, we will explore a **case study** where we deploy a **sentiment analysis model** as an API.

Introduction to Model Deployment

Once a machine learning model has been trained and evaluated, the next step is to deploy it so it can be used in a production environment. **Model deployment** involves:

1. **Saving the trained model**: Converting the model into a format that can be stored and used later.

2. **Loading the model**: Restoring the saved model for inference or prediction.

3. **Serving the model**: Making the model available through an API or as part of an application, allowing users or systems to interact with the model.

Deployment ensures that your model can make predictions in real time or in batch, based on new incoming data.

Saving and Loading Models in Python using Joblib and Pickle

Once you've trained a machine learning model, you need to **save** it so it can be reused later without retraining. Python provides several libraries to handle model serialization, with **joblib** and **pickle** being two of the most popular.

1. Saving and Loading Models with Joblib

Joblib is a popular Python library used for saving large objects such as machine learning models. It is more efficient than **pickle** when working with models that contain large numerical arrays, as it uses a more efficient binary format.

- **Saving a model**:

```
python
```

```
import joblib
from        sklearn.ensemble        import
RandomForestClassifier

# Train a model
model = RandomForestClassifier()
model.fit(X_train, y_train)

# Save the model to a file
joblib.dump(model, 'random_forest_model.pkl')
```

- **Loading a model**:

```
python

# Load the model from the file
loaded_model                                =
joblib.load('random_forest_model.pkl')

# Use the model to make predictions
predictions = loaded_model.predict(X_test)
```

2. Saving and Loading Models with Pickle

Pickle is another popular Python library for serializing objects. It is a general-purpose serialization library, and while it works well for most objects, it may be less efficient than **joblib** for large numerical arrays.

- **Saving a model**:

228

```python
python

import pickle

# Train a model
model = RandomForestClassifier()
model.fit(X_train, y_train)

# Save the model to a file
with open('random_forest_model.pkl', 'wb') as f:
    pickle.dump(model, f)
```

- **Loading a model**:

```python
python

# Load the model from the file
with open('random_forest_model.pkl', 'rb') as f:
    loaded_model = pickle.load(f)

# Use the model to make predictions
predictions = loaded_model.predict(X_test)
```

Both **joblib** and **pickle** allow you to persist models so they can be deployed and used in production environments without needing to retrain them each time.

229

Deploying Models Using Flask or FastAPI for Web Services

To make a model accessible over the web, we can deploy it as an API. **Flask** and **FastAPI** are two popular Python web frameworks for building APIs. In both cases, we'll create a simple web service that loads the model and serves predictions.

1. Deploying with Flask

Flask is a lightweight web framework for building APIs in Python. It's easy to set up and use, making it a great choice for model deployment.

- **Step 1: Install Flask**

bash

```bash
pip install flask
```

- **Step 2: Create a Flask API for Model Deployment**

Here is an example of how to deploy a trained machine learning model using Flask:

python

```python
from flask import Flask, request, jsonify
import joblib
```

```python
app = Flask(__name__)

# Load the model
model = joblib.load('random_forest_model.pkl')

@app.route('/predict', methods=['POST'])
def predict():
    # Get the data from the POST request
    data = request.get_json(force=True)
    # Extract features from the data
    features = data['features']

    # Make prediction using the model
    prediction = model.predict([features])

    # Return the prediction as a JSON response
    return                jsonify({'prediction':
prediction[0]})

if __name__ == '__main__':
    app.run(debug=True)
```

- **Step 3: Start the Flask server**

Run the Flask app by executing the script. The API will be available at http://127.0.0.1:5000/ by default.

231

To make a prediction, you can send a **POST** request to `http://127.0.0.1:5000/predict` with JSON data containing the features.

```bash
```

```bash
curl -X POST -H "Content-Type: application/json"
-d '{"features": [5.1, 3.5, 1.4, 0.2]}'
http://127.0.0.1:5000/predict
```

2. Deploying with FastAPI

FastAPI is another modern Python web framework that is faster than Flask due to its asynchronous capabilities. It's also more suited for APIs that require high performance.

- **Step 1: Install FastAPI and Uvicorn**

```bash
```

```bash
pip install fastapi uvicorn
```

- **Step 2: Create a FastAPI API for Model Deployment**

Here's an example of deploying the model with FastAPI:

```python
```

```python
from fastapi import FastAPI
from pydantic import BaseModel
```

232

```
import joblib

app = FastAPI()

# Load the model
model = joblib.load('random_forest_model.pkl')

# Define the input data model
class InputData(BaseModel):
    features: list

@app.post("/predict")
def predict(data: InputData):
    # Make prediction using the model
    prediction = model.predict([data.features])

    # Return the prediction as a JSON response
    return {"prediction": int(prediction[0])}

if __name__ == '__main__':
    import uvicorn
    uvicorn.run(app,           host="127.0.0.1",
port=8000)
```

- **Step 3: Start the FastAPI server**

Run the FastAPI app with **Uvicorn**:

```
bash
```

233

```
uvicorn app:app --reload
```

The FastAPI server will be running at http://127.0.0.1:8000/. To make a prediction, you can send a **POST** request with the input features:

```bash
bash
```

```
curl -X 'POST' \
  'http://127.0.0.1:8000/predict' \
  -H 'Content-Type: application/json' \
  -d '{
  "features": [5.1, 3.5, 1.4, 0.2]
}'
```

Using Cloud Platforms Like AWS and Google Cloud for Deployment

For deploying models in production at scale, cloud platforms like **AWS** and **Google Cloud** provide robust infrastructure and tools for serving models.

1. AWS (Amazon Web Services)

AWS offers several services for deploying machine learning models:

- **Amazon SageMaker**: A fully managed service that provides tools to build, train, and deploy machine learning

234

models at scale. You can deploy models directly from Jupyter notebooks to SageMaker endpoints for real-time predictions.

- **AWS Lambda**: Serverless compute service for deploying lightweight models and making predictions on the fly.

2. Google Cloud Platform (GCP)

Google Cloud offers several tools for deploying machine learning models:

- **AI Platform**: Managed service for training and deploying models at scale. It supports deployment of models as **REST APIs** for serving predictions.
- **Cloud Functions**: Serverless compute service, similar to AWS Lambda, for deploying lightweight models.

Case Study: Deploying a Sentiment Analysis Model as an API

In this case study, we'll deploy a simple **sentiment analysis** model using **Flask** or **FastAPI**. The model will classify text as either positive or negative.

Step 1: Train the Sentiment Analysis Model

For simplicity, we will use a pre-trained model, such as a **Logistic Regression** model trained on a sentiment analysis dataset.

```python
python

from sklearn.datasets import load_files
from sklearn.feature_extraction.text import TfidfVectorizer
from sklearn.linear_model import LogisticRegression
import joblib

# Load the dataset
reviews = load_files('txt_sentoken')
X, y = reviews.data, reviews.target

# Vectorize the text data
vectorizer = TfidfVectorizer()
X_vect = vectorizer.fit_transform(X)

# Train the model
model = LogisticRegression()
model.fit(X_vect, y)

# Save the model and vectorizer
joblib.dump(model, 'sentiment_model.pkl')
joblib.dump(vectorizer, 'vectorizer.pkl')
```

Step 2: Create the API

We'll create an API to accept text input and return the sentiment prediction.

Flask API:

```python
from flask import Flask, request, jsonify
import joblib

app = Flask(__name__)

# Load the model and vectorizer
model = joblib.load('sentiment_model.pkl')
vectorizer = joblib.load('vectorizer.pkl')

@app.route('/predict', methods=['POST'])
def predict():
    data = request.get_json()
    text = data['text']
    text_vect = vectorizer.transform([text])
    prediction = model.predict(text_vect)
    sentiment = 'positive' if prediction == 1
else 'negative'
    return jsonify({'sentiment': sentiment})

if __name__ == '__main__':
    app.run(debug=True)
```

FastAPI API:

python

```python
from fastapi import FastAPI
from pydantic import BaseModel
import joblib

app = FastAPI()

# Load the model and vectorizer
model = joblib.load('sentiment_model.pkl')
vectorizer = joblib.load('vectorizer.pkl')

class TextInput(BaseModel):
    text: str

@app.post("/predict")
def predict(data: TextInput):
    text_vect                          =
vectorizer.transform([data.text])
    prediction = model.predict(text_vect)
    sentiment = 'positive' if prediction == 1
else 'negative'
    return {"sentiment": sentiment}
```

Step 3: Deploy the API

Follow the steps outlined for deploying the model with **Flask** or **FastAPI**. You can deploy the model locally or to a cloud platform for production use.

Key Takeaways

- **Model deployment** allows your trained machine learning models to make predictions in real-time or on-demand through APIs.

- **Saving and loading models** with libraries like **joblib** and **pickle** makes it easy to persist and reuse models.

- **Flask** and **FastAPI** are popular frameworks for deploying models as APIs, allowing users to interact with the model over the web.

- Cloud platforms like **AWS** and **Google Cloud** provide scalable infrastructure for deploying models in production environments.

- In the **case study**, we deployed a simple **sentiment analysis model** as an API using Flask or FastAPI.

In the next chapter, we will explore **advanced deployment strategies**, including deploying models in **serverless environments** and using **containerization** technologies like **Docker** for scalability and flexibility.

239

CHAPTER 21

ETHICS AND FAIRNESS IN AI

In this chapter, we will dive into the important and increasingly relevant topic of **ethics** and **fairness** in **artificial intelligence (AI)**. As AI systems become more integrated into society, they have the potential to affect many aspects of human life. From hiring decisions to law enforcement, AI systems can influence individuals and communities in profound ways. This chapter will address the challenges of **bias, ethical considerations, fairness,** and **privacy** in AI development, as well as how to ensure these systems operate in a transparent and responsible manner. We will also walk through a **case study** that focuses on **identifying and mitigating bias** in machine learning models.

Understanding Bias in AI Models

Bias in AI refers to the systematic and unfair discrimination against certain groups or individuals, often based on characteristics like race, gender, or socioeconomic status. Bias can arise in AI systems at various stages: from the data collection process to model training and even in the design of algorithms. These biases can result in unfair and discriminatory outcomes, reinforcing societal inequalities.

1. Sources of Bias

- **Data Bias**: If the training data is not representative of the real-world population, the model will learn biased patterns. For instance, if a facial recognition system is trained primarily on images of light-skinned individuals, it may perform poorly on individuals with darker skin tones.
- **Algorithmic Bias**: Even if the data is unbiased, algorithms themselves can introduce bias. This can occur if the algorithm amplifies certain patterns or underrepresents others based on how the model is structured.
- **Human Bias**: Bias can also stem from the developers themselves. For example, developers' own beliefs and assumptions can unintentionally affect the way they design and implement AI systems.

2. Types of Bias in AI

- **Selection Bias**: Occurs when the data used to train the model is not representative of the target population. For example, if a loan approval algorithm is trained on data from a specific region, it may perform poorly for people from other regions.
- **Sampling Bias**: Occurs when certain segments of the population are over- or under-sampled. For instance, a

medical diagnostic model trained on data from one age group may not generalize well to others.

- **Label Bias**: In supervised learning, labels are provided by humans. If these labels are biased, the model will learn biased patterns. For example, if a dataset used to train a sentiment analysis model contains biased labels (e.g., labeling negative sentiment for certain groups), the model will inherit that bias.

Ethical Considerations in AI Development

As AI systems become more pervasive, it is crucial to consider their ethical implications. Ethical considerations help guide the responsible development and deployment of AI technologies.

1. Autonomy and Control

AI systems should respect human autonomy and ensure that individuals remain in control of important decisions. AI should not replace human decision-making but instead assist in decision-making processes, providing recommendations and insights that can improve outcomes.

2. Accountability and Responsibility

Developers and organizations that create AI systems must be accountable for the outcomes. This includes taking responsibility

242

for harmful decisions made by AI systems, whether the harm is intentional or unintentional.

3. Transparency and Explainability

AI systems should be transparent, and their decision-making processes should be explainable. **Explainability** allows stakeholders to understand how and why a model arrived at a particular decision, which is crucial for building trust and ensuring fairness.

- For example, in healthcare, if an AI system recommends a particular treatment, the rationale behind the recommendation should be clearly explained to medical professionals, who can then decide whether to follow the advice.

4. Preventing Harm

AI development should prioritize minimizing harm. This includes addressing concerns related to the unintended consequences of AI systems, such as reinforcing negative stereotypes, amplifying inequalities, or making decisions that disproportionately harm vulnerable groups.

Ensuring Fairness and Transparency in AI Systems

To ensure that AI systems are fair and transparent, we must take proactive steps during their design, development, and deployment.

1. Fairness in AI

Fairness in AI refers to the idea that AI systems should not produce discriminatory outcomes, regardless of the group characteristics of the individuals affected. Ensuring fairness requires careful consideration of the data, the model's behavior, and the outcomes.

- **Fairness through awareness**: Recognizing and addressing known biases in the data and algorithms. For example, if a hiring algorithm is shown to disproportionately favor male candidates, it's crucial to adjust the model to ensure it evaluates candidates fairly regardless of gender.
- **Fairness through outcomes**: Evaluating the outcomes of an AI system to ensure it does not disproportionately harm certain groups. Metrics like **demographic parity** or **equal opportunity** can be used to assess fairness.

2. Transparency in AI

Transparency ensures that AI systems are understandable and that stakeholders can trust how decisions are made. This includes:

244

- **Model explainability**: Making the workings of the model interpretable to users.

- **Auditable decision-making**: Enabling external audits of the model's predictions to assess fairness, accuracy, and ethical adherence.

Transparency also helps identify where things go wrong and allows for adjustments if necessary.

Privacy Concerns and Data Protection in AI

AI systems often require large amounts of personal data to train effectively, which raises significant privacy concerns. Protecting users' privacy and ensuring their data is handled responsibly is critical to building trustworthy AI systems.

1. Data Privacy

Data privacy refers to the rights of individuals to control their personal information and how it is used. In the context of AI, this means ensuring that personal data used to train models is anonymized and protected from unauthorized access or misuse.

2. GDPR and AI

The **General Data Protection Regulation (GDPR)** is a regulation in the European Union aimed at protecting individuals' privacy and data. GDPR applies to AI systems in several ways, including the right to **explainability** (the right to understand how decisions are made), **data minimization** (limiting the amount of data collected), and **consent** (ensuring users consent to the use of their data).

3. Differential Privacy

Differential privacy is a technique used to ensure that individual data points cannot be re-identified in datasets. It adds noise to the data or results, ensuring that an individual's data cannot be distinguished from others, thus protecting privacy even in large datasets.

Case Study: Identifying and Mitigating Bias in Machine Learning

In this case study, we will explore how to identify and mitigate bias in a machine learning model, specifically focusing on a **loan approval model** that predicts whether a loan application will be approved based on features such as income, credit score, and age.

Step 1: Analyze the Data for Bias

Start by analyzing the training data for any potential bias. For example, if the data is imbalanced with respect to gender or race, it could lead to biased predictions.

```python

import pandas as pd

# Load the dataset
df = pd.read_csv('loan_data.csv')

# Check for imbalance in gender and race
print(df['gender'].value_counts())
print(df['race'].value_counts())
```

Step 2: Evaluate the Model's Fairness

Next, evaluate the fairness of the model by checking whether its predictions disproportionately favor one group over others.

```python

from sklearn.metrics import confusion_matrix

# Assuming we have the true labels (y_true) and
model predictions (y_pred)
conf_matrix = confusion_matrix(y_true, y_pred)
print(conf_matrix)

# Evaluate fairness based on demographic groups
(e.g., gender, race)
# Check if certain groups have higher false
positives or false negatives
```

Step 3: Mitigate Bias Using Fairness Techniques

To mitigate bias, we can apply fairness techniques, such as:

- **Re-sampling**: Adjust the training dataset to ensure balanced representation of different groups.
- **Fairness constraints**: Add fairness constraints to the training process, ensuring that the model's predictions are unbiased across demographic groups.

```python
from sklearn.utils import import resample

# Re-sample the minority group to balance the
dataset
minority_group = df[df['gender'] == 'female']
majority_group = df[df['gender'] == 'male']

minority_resampled = resample(minority_group,
replace=True, n_samples=len(majority_group),
random_state=42)

# Combine the resampled minority group with the
majority group
df_balanced = pd.concat([majority_group,
minority_resampled])
```

Step 4: Re-train and Evaluate the Model

After mitigating bias, re-train the model on the balanced dataset and evaluate its fairness again.

Key Takeaways

- **Bias** in AI models can arise from various sources, such as biased data, algorithms, or human influences. It's crucial to identify and address bias to ensure fairness.
- **Ethical considerations** in AI development include ensuring transparency, accountability, and fairness, as well as minimizing harm to vulnerable groups.
- **Privacy** concerns in AI are significant, and techniques like **differential privacy** and adherence to regulations like **GDPR** are essential for protecting user data.
- In the **case study**, we demonstrated how to identify and mitigate bias in a machine learning model using fairness techniques like **resampling**.

In the next chapter, we will explore **advanced topics** in AI deployment, including deploying models in **distributed systems** and **serverless environments** for real-time inference.

CHAPTER 22

AI IN BUSINESS AND INDUSTRY

In this chapter, we will explore the profound impact of **Artificial Intelligence (AI)** across various industries. AI is transforming business operations by enabling smarter decision-making, enhancing efficiency, and delivering new insights. We will look at **AI applications in industries** such as **healthcare, finance**, and **retail**, and discuss how AI can be used for **predictive analytics**, **decision-making**, and building **recommendation systems**. We will also examine **real-world case studies** to illustrate how businesses are leveraging AI to innovate and improve operations.

AI Applications in Various Industries: Healthcare, Finance, Retail, and More

AI has a wide range of applications across multiple sectors, enabling businesses to streamline operations, improve customer service, and gain competitive advantages. Below, we highlight how AI is being used in several key industries.

1. Healthcare

In healthcare, AI is revolutionizing everything from diagnosis and treatment to patient care and administrative tasks. Some of the most prominent applications of AI in healthcare include:

- **Medical Imaging**: AI models, particularly **Convolutional Neural Networks (CNNs)**, are used to analyze medical images such as X-rays, MRIs, and CT scans. These models can detect abnormalities such as tumors, fractures, and other medical conditions, sometimes with higher accuracy than human radiologists.
- **Predictive Analytics**: AI models are used to predict patient outcomes, such as the likelihood of readmission, disease progression, and response to treatment. By analyzing historical patient data, AI helps healthcare providers make more informed decisions.
- **Drug Discovery**: AI speeds up the process of discovering new drugs by analyzing large datasets of biological information and identifying potential drug candidates more efficiently than traditional methods.
- **Personalized Medicine**: AI models are used to tailor treatments based on an individual's genetic makeup, lifestyle, and other factors, improving the effectiveness of treatments.

251

2. Finance

In the finance industry, AI plays a crucial role in streamlining operations, improving decision-making, and enhancing customer experiences. Some key AI applications in finance include:

- **Fraud Detection**: AI is used to analyze transactional data in real-time and identify potentially fraudulent activities. Machine learning models can detect unusual patterns in spending and flag suspicious transactions.

- **Algorithmic Trading**: AI models, including **deep learning** and **reinforcement learning**, are used to execute trades at optimal times based on market conditions, historical data, and predictive signals. These models can make high-frequency trades, potentially outperforming human traders.

- **Credit Scoring and Risk Assessment**: AI-powered models assess creditworthiness by analyzing historical financial data, including transaction history and behavioral patterns, to predict the likelihood of a borrower defaulting on a loan.

3. Retail

AI is transforming the retail industry by improving customer experiences, optimizing inventory management, and enhancing sales strategies. Some prominent AI applications in retail include:

- **Recommendation Systems**: AI-driven recommendation systems, such as those used by Amazon and Netflix, suggest products or services based on customer behavior, preferences, and previous purchases.

- **Personalized Marketing**: AI helps businesses deliver personalized marketing campaigns by analyzing consumer data and predicting the types of products or services a customer is likely to purchase.

- **Inventory Management**: AI systems are used to optimize inventory levels by predicting demand, reducing waste, and ensuring products are available when needed.

- **Chatbots and Virtual Assistants**: AI-powered chatbots provide customers with 24/7 support, answering inquiries, assisting with purchases, and guiding users through websites or apps.

4. Manufacturing and Supply Chain

AI is increasingly being used in manufacturing to improve efficiency, optimize supply chains, and reduce costs:

- **Predictive Maintenance**: AI models predict when machines will fail based on sensor data, allowing businesses to perform maintenance before costly breakdowns occur.

253

- **Supply Chain Optimization**: AI helps optimize supply chains by predicting demand, improving routing logistics, and identifying the most efficient suppliers or routes.

5. Transportation and Autonomous Vehicles

AI is enabling the development of autonomous vehicles, optimizing traffic management, and improving transportation systems:

- **Autonomous Vehicles**: AI is at the core of self-driving car technology, helping vehicles recognize objects, navigate safely, and make decisions in real-time.
- **Route Optimization**: AI-powered systems optimize traffic flow, predict congestion, and find the most efficient routes for delivery vehicles or public transportation.

Using AI for Predictive Analytics and Decision-Making

AI is a powerful tool for predictive analytics, helping businesses forecast future trends, customer behavior, and other important metrics. Predictive models, often built using machine learning algorithms, analyze historical data and generate insights that guide decision-making. Below are examples of how AI is used for predictive analytics:

254

1. Predictive Maintenance

In manufacturing and transportation, AI models are used to predict when equipment will fail, allowing for proactive maintenance. This helps reduce downtime, save on repairs, and extend the life of assets.

2. Customer Churn Prediction

AI models analyze customer behavior to predict whether a customer is likely to leave a service or stop purchasing products. By identifying at-risk customers, businesses can implement retention strategies, such as personalized offers or loyalty programs.

3. Demand Forecasting

AI models predict product demand based on historical sales data, market trends, and other relevant factors. This helps businesses optimize inventory levels, reduce costs, and avoid stockouts or overstocking.

4. Dynamic Pricing

AI-powered pricing models analyze market conditions, competitor prices, and customer behavior to dynamically adjust the prices of products or services. This helps businesses maximize revenue while staying competitive.

Building AI-powered Recommendation Systems

Recommendation systems are among the most widely used AI applications in industries like retail, entertainment, and social media. These systems suggest products, movies, music, or content based on user preferences and behavior.

Types of Recommendation Systems:

- **Collaborative Filtering**: This approach relies on user-item interactions. For example, it recommends products based on what similar users have liked or purchased. It can be further divided into:
    - **User-based collaborative filtering**: Recommending items liked by similar users.
    - **Item-based collaborative filtering**: Recommending items that are similar to items the user has liked or interacted with.
- **Content-based Filtering**: This method recommends items based on the characteristics of the items and a user's preferences. For example, recommending movies based on the genres, directors, or actors a user has watched in the past.
- **Hybrid Systems**: These systems combine multiple recommendation techniques to improve accuracy and handle limitations of individual methods.

256

Building a Simple Collaborative Filtering Model (Using Python)

python

```python
import pandas as pd
from sklearn.neighbors import NearestNeighbors

# Sample data: user-item interaction matrix
(users vs products)
data = {'Product A': [1, 0, 1, 0, 0],
        'Product B': [0, 1, 1, 0, 0],
        'Product C': [1, 1, 0, 1, 0],
        'Product D': [0, 1, 1, 1, 1]}

# Convert to a DataFrame
df = pd.DataFrame(data, index=['User1', 'User2',
'User3', 'User4', 'User5'])

# Use Nearest Neighbors to find similar users
(Collaborative Filtering)
model = NearestNeighbors(n_neighbors=3)
model.fit(df.T)   # Transpose the matrix to use
products as features
distances,              indices              =
model.kneighbors(df['Product
A'].values.reshape(1, -1))

# Recommended users based on Product A
print(f"Users similar to the user who liked
Product A: {df.index[indices.flatten()]}")
```

257

Real-World Case Studies of AI in Business

1. Netflix's Recommendation System

Netflix uses a complex hybrid recommendation system to suggest movies and TV shows to its users. By analyzing user behavior, such as the genres, actors, and movies watched, Netflix is able to personalize recommendations for each user, keeping them engaged and improving user satisfaction.

2. Amazon's Personalized Shopping Experience

Amazon's recommendation system is based on collaborative filtering, suggesting products based on what similar users have bought or what products are commonly purchased together. It's a key driver behind Amazon's success, as it increases sales by recommending products that users are most likely to purchase.

3. Google Search Algorithms

Google uses AI-powered algorithms to rank search results based on relevance. By analyzing user behavior, clicks, and search history, Google can serve personalized search results that match a user's intent, making the search experience more effective.

4. IBM Watson in Healthcare

IBM Watson uses AI to analyze vast amounts of medical data, including patient records, clinical trial data, and medical literature. It helps doctors make more informed decisions, suggest treatments, and assist with diagnoses, improving patient outcomes and operational efficiency.

How AI Can Transform Industries and Improve Operations

AI has the potential to transform nearly every industry by enhancing efficiency, automating processes, and enabling smarter decision-making. Here are a few key ways AI is improving operations:

- **Automation**: AI automates routine and repetitive tasks, freeing up employees to focus on more creative and high-value work.
- **Real-time Decision Making**: AI systems provide real-time insights that allow businesses to make decisions quickly and efficiently, such as dynamic pricing or inventory optimization.
- **Cost Savings**: AI improves operational efficiency, reducing costs associated with human labor, waste, and errors.

- **Customer Satisfaction**: Personalized experiences powered by AI help improve customer satisfaction by delivering relevant products, services, and support.

Key Takeaways

- **AI is transforming industries** by automating tasks, improving decision-making, and enabling new business models.

- **Applications of AI in various industries** include healthcare (diagnosis and drug discovery), finance (fraud detection and algorithmic trading), retail (recommendation systems and personalized marketing), and more.

- **Predictive analytics** powered by AI helps businesses forecast future trends, optimize operations, and improve customer experiences.

- **AI-powered recommendation systems** use collaborative filtering, content-based filtering, and hybrid models to suggest relevant products or services.

- **Case studies** demonstrate how companies like Netflix, Amazon, and IBM are using AI to revolutionize their industries and improve their operations.

In the next chapter, we will explore **AI integration with IoT (Internet of Things)**, focusing on how AI is being used to analyze data from smart devices and optimize performance in real-time systems.

CHAPTER 23

CHALLENGES IN AI DEVELOPMENT

AI development presents numerous challenges, from ensuring high-quality data to maintaining models over time and deploying them in production environments. In this chapter, we will explore some of the most common challenges faced during AI development, including **data quality and availability**, **scaling AI models**, **model drift**, **deployment issues**, and the difficulty of working with **unsupervised learning** when labeled data is scarce. Understanding and addressing these challenges is crucial for building robust, scalable, and effective AI systems.

Data Quality and Availability Challenges

One of the biggest hurdles in AI development is ensuring that the data used to train models is of **high quality** and readily available. AI systems are heavily reliant on large amounts of data, and any issues with data quality can have a significant impact on the performance of the model.

1. Missing or Incomplete Data

Data used in training AI models can often be incomplete or contain missing values. For example, in healthcare datasets, some patient records may be missing important information like age or medical history, which can lead to poor model performance.

- **Solution**: Techniques like **imputation** (replacing missing values with estimates) or using **data augmentation** (generating additional data points) can help address missing data.

2. Noisy Data

Data can also contain noise—irrelevant or random information that doesn't contribute to the learning process. For example, in financial data, minor fluctuations in stock prices may be incorrectly interpreted as significant patterns by an AI model.

- **Solution**: Data preprocessing techniques, such as **smoothing**, **filtering**, or **outlier detection**, can help reduce noise in the dataset.

3. Imbalanced Data

In many real-world scenarios, the data is imbalanced, meaning that certain classes are underrepresented. For example, in fraud detection, fraudulent transactions may be far less frequent than legitimate ones, causing the model to learn biased patterns.

- **Solution**: Techniques like **resampling, SMOTE (Synthetic Minority Over-sampling Technique)**, and **class weighting** can be used to address data imbalance.

4. Data Availability

In certain fields, acquiring high-quality labeled data can be expensive or time-consuming. For instance, in medical imaging, obtaining labeled data requires expert annotations, which may not always be readily available.

- **Solution**: **Transfer learning** (using pre-trained models on similar tasks) and **synthetic data generation** (creating artificial data for training) can help address data availability issues.

Scaling AI Models to Large Datasets

As the scale of AI applications grows, so does the volume of data. Scaling AI models to handle large datasets efficiently is a critical challenge in AI development.

1. Computational Resources

Training large-scale AI models requires significant computational resources, including powerful hardware like **GPUs** or **TPUs**. Handling these resources at scale can be costly and may require sophisticated cloud infrastructure.

- **Solution**: Using **cloud platforms** (such as AWS, Google Cloud, or Microsoft Azure) provides scalable infrastructure for training large models. **Distributed computing** frameworks, such as **Apache Spark**, can also be used to handle large datasets in parallel across multiple machines.

2. Model Complexity

As datasets grow in size, AI models also become more complex, leading to challenges in training time, overfitting, and model interpretability. Complex models with millions of parameters may be prone to overfitting when trained on limited data.

- **Solution**: Techniques like **model pruning**, **parameter sharing**, and using more **efficient architectures** (e.g., lightweight neural networks) can help manage model complexity and reduce overfitting.

3. Data Pipeline Optimization

Efficient data processing pipelines are essential for handling large datasets. Without optimized data ingestion, preprocessing, and transformation pipelines, training AI models can become a bottleneck.

- **Solution**: Implementing **streaming data pipelines**, using **distributed data storage systems** (e.g., Hadoop, Spark), and automating data preprocessing steps can ensure faster data handling and model training.

Handling Model Drift and Updating Models Over Time

Once a model is deployed, it is critical to ensure that it continues to perform well as new data comes in. **Model drift**, or **concept drift**, refers to changes in the data distribution over time, which can make previously trained models less accurate.

1. Types of Model Drift

- **Data Drift**: The input data distribution changes over time, which may lead to the model receiving different types of inputs than it was trained on.
- **Concept Drift**: The relationship between the input data and the target variable changes over time, leading to incorrect predictions.

266

2. Monitoring and Detection

Monitoring the performance of models in production is essential to detect model drift. This can be done by comparing the **model's performance** on recent data to its performance on the original training data.

- **Solution**: Implementing **continuous monitoring** systems and using **drift detection algorithms** (such as **Kolmogorov-Smirnov test** or **population stability index**) helps identify when drift is occurring.

3. Updating Models

When model drift is detected, the model must be retrained on new data to reflect the changes in the environment or data. Continuous **model retraining** is a key aspect of maintaining AI systems.

- **Solution**: Establish a **model retraining pipeline** to automate the retraining process and deploy updated models without significant downtime.

The Challenges of Deploying AI in Production

Deploying AI models into production comes with its own set of challenges that require careful planning and execution. AI models often work well in controlled environments (e.g., in research or

267

during development), but they can face unforeseen difficulties when used in real-world applications.

1. Model Integration

Integrating an AI model with existing production systems can be difficult, especially in large organizations with complex IT architectures. Ensuring smooth communication between the model and other systems is crucial for operational efficiency.

- **Solution**: Using **containerization** (with **Docker**), **API development** (with **Flask** or **FastAPI**), and **model versioning** (with **MLflow** or **DVC**) can help integrate AI models smoothly into production pipelines.

2. Latency and Performance

In real-time applications, such as fraud detection or autonomous driving, low-latency predictions are essential. Models that are too slow can hinder the system's performance and impact user experience.

- **Solution**: Optimizing models for **low-latency inference**, using hardware acceleration (like **TPUs**), and applying **model compression** techniques (such as **quantization** and **pruning**) can reduce latency.

268

3. Security and Privacy Concerns

AI systems often process sensitive data (e.g., health records or financial information), which raises significant privacy and security concerns. Ensuring data protection while maintaining high model performance is a delicate balance.

- **Solution**: Implementing **encryption**, **access control**, and **differential privacy** techniques ensures data security. **Federated learning** can also be used to train models without transferring sensitive data from users to servers.

Overcoming the Lack of Labeled Data in Unsupervised Learning

In many real-world applications, acquiring labeled data is time-consuming, costly, or infeasible. This presents a significant challenge for training supervised learning models, which require a large amount of labeled data.

1. Unsupervised Learning

In **unsupervised learning**, the model is trained without labeled data. Instead, it tries to find patterns, clusters, or representations from the input data. Common techniques include:

- **Clustering** (e.g., **K-means**, **DBSCAN**).
- **Dimensionality reduction** (e.g., **PCA**, **t-SNE**).

- **Anomaly detection**.

2. Semi-supervised Learning

Semi-supervised learning combines both labeled and unlabeled data, making use of a small amount of labeled data and a larger amount of unlabeled data. This approach is particularly useful when labeling is expensive.

- **Solution**: Techniques such as **self-training, co-training,** and **graph-based methods** can help improve the performance of semi-supervised learning models.

3. Transfer Learning

Transfer learning allows models to leverage knowledge gained from one domain (where labeled data is available) and apply it to another domain (where labeled data is scarce). This is particularly useful when labeled data is limited but similar datasets exist.

- **Solution**: **Pre-trained models** (e.g., **BERT** for text or **ResNet** for images) can be fine-tuned on the target domain with less labeled data.

Key Takeaways

- **Data quality** and availability are key challenges in AI development. Ensuring high-quality, representative data is essential for training effective models.

- **Scaling AI models** to handle large datasets requires robust computational resources and efficient data pipelines.

- **Model drift** is a common issue in production, requiring continuous monitoring and updates to maintain model accuracy over time.

- **Deployment in production** requires careful integration, attention to performance and latency, and addressing security and privacy concerns.

- **Unsupervised learning** and **semi-supervised learning** can be used to overcome the lack of labeled data, with techniques like transfer learning providing effective solutions.

In the next chapter, we will explore **AI-driven automation**, focusing on how AI can automate business processes, improve efficiency, and drive innovation in various industries.

271

CHAPTER 24

FUTURE TRENDS IN AI

As AI continues to evolve at a rapid pace, it is increasingly shaping the future of technology and transforming various industries. In this chapter, we will explore some of the key **future trends in AI**, including its growing role in **automation**, the rise of **autonomous systems** like self-driving cars and drones, and the intersection of AI with other **emerging technologies** such as **blockchain**, **Internet of Things (IoT)**, and **quantum computing**. We will also offer some **predictions** for the future of AI and machine learning.

The Role of AI in Shaping the Future of Technology

AI is poised to become the backbone of many future technological advancements. It is already a core component of systems that analyze massive datasets, automate tasks, and make intelligent decisions. As AI systems become more sophisticated, they will continue to drive innovation across a variety of sectors.

1. Intelligent Automation

AI's role in automation is growing, and it is expected to expand significantly in the coming years. By automating complex tasks,

272

AI will not only improve productivity but also allow humans to focus on more creative and high-value work. For example, AI-powered **Robotic Process Automation (RPA)** is already being used to automate repetitive administrative tasks, while **AI-driven chatbots** handle customer support inquiries.

2. Personalized Technology

AI will continue to enhance personalization across various fields, from **healthcare** (personalized treatments and diagnostic tools) to **retail** (customized shopping experiences). As AI systems become more capable of understanding individual preferences, they will power **personalized recommendations** that adapt to users' needs in real-time, making interactions with technology more intuitive and user-centric.

3. Smart Cities and Infrastructure

AI will play a crucial role in the development of **smart cities** by optimizing energy use, improving traffic management, and enhancing public services. Smart infrastructure powered by AI will allow cities to manage resources more efficiently, reduce environmental impact, and improve the quality of life for residents.

AI and Automation in the Workforce

AI is already impacting the workforce, automating many routine tasks and augmenting human capabilities. However, the rise of AI and automation also raises questions about the future of jobs and the economy.

1. The Changing Nature of Work

As AI and automation take over more repetitive and manual tasks, the demand for roles focused on **creativity**, **problem-solving**, and **emotional intelligence** will rise. Jobs that require human judgment, empathy, and complex decision-making will become more valuable. For example, healthcare professionals, educators, and creative designers will continue to work alongside AI to enhance outcomes.

2. Job Displacement and Creation

While some jobs will inevitably be displaced by AI-driven automation, new opportunities will emerge in sectors such as AI development, data science, robotics, and AI ethics. Governments and organizations must focus on **reskilling** and **upskilling** workers to prepare them for these emerging roles. Additionally, AI can help in creating better work environments by eliminating dangerous and physically demanding tasks.

3. AI in Decision-Making

AI is increasingly being used to augment decision-making in businesses and organizations. For example, **AI-powered analytics tools** can analyze vast amounts of data to provide insights that help managers make better decisions faster. In the future, AI systems will work alongside human decision-makers, offering recommendations and predictions that enable more efficient operations.

The Rise of Autonomous Systems: Self-Driving Cars, Drones, and Robots

Autonomous systems powered by AI are among the most exciting developments shaping the future of technology. These systems have the potential to revolutionize industries such as transportation, logistics, and healthcare.

1. Self-Driving Cars

Self-driving cars, powered by AI, are one of the most high-profile applications of autonomous systems. These cars use AI algorithms to process data from sensors (such as cameras, LIDAR, and radar) and make real-time decisions about navigation, traffic, and obstacle avoidance. The widespread adoption of autonomous vehicles has the potential to reduce traffic accidents, lower emissions, and revolutionize the transportation industry.

- **Challenges**: While significant progress has been made in autonomous driving technology, there are still challenges to overcome, such as safety concerns, regulatory approval, and the integration of self-driving cars with existing road infrastructures.

2. Drones

AI-powered drones are already being used in various industries, from **delivery services** to **agriculture** and **disaster relief**. These drones can autonomously navigate and complete tasks such as inspecting infrastructure, delivering packages, or surveying agricultural land for crop health.

- **Future Potential**: In the future, AI-driven drones could be widely used for autonomous delivery, real-time monitoring of environmental changes, and even emergency response in situations where human intervention would be too dangerous.

3. Robotics

AI-driven robots are transforming industries by performing tasks that require precision, dexterity, and decision-making capabilities. In manufacturing, **collaborative robots (cobots)** work alongside human workers to handle dangerous tasks or perform repetitive actions. In healthcare, robots are already being used for surgeries and rehabilitation.

- **Future Potential**: The evolution of robots powered by AI could result in fully autonomous robots that operate in complex environments, such as hospitals, homes, and offices, carrying out everything from cleaning to caregiving.

The Intersection of AI with Other Emerging Technologies: Blockchain, IoT, and Quantum Computing

AI is not an isolated field; it intersects with other cutting-edge technologies, creating new possibilities and enhancing capabilities.

1. AI and Blockchain

Blockchain is a decentralized, distributed ledger technology that ensures transparency, security, and immutability of data. When combined with AI, blockchain can enhance AI systems by ensuring data integrity and reducing risks related to **data manipulation** or **fraud**. Moreover, AI can be used to optimize blockchain systems by improving consensus algorithms or predicting transaction behaviors.

2. AI and the Internet of Things (IoT)

The **Internet of Things (IoT)** refers to the network of connected devices that communicate and exchange data. AI can enhance IoT by enabling devices to make autonomous decisions based on real-time data. For instance, smart thermostats, powered by AI, can learn user preferences and optimize energy consumption in real-time. In the future, AI could power **intelligent IoT networks** where devices collaborate and make decisions without human intervention.

3. AI and Quantum Computing

Quantum computing is an emerging field that leverages the principles of quantum mechanics to solve complex problems at unprecedented speeds. AI can benefit from quantum computing by processing large datasets and running highly complex simulations much faster than classical computers. As quantum computing continues to develop, we can expect AI models to be trained faster and to solve more intricate problems, opening up new areas for AI applications in science, healthcare, and cryptography.

Predictions for the Future of AI and Machine Learning

As AI continues to advance, its impact on the world will only increase. Here are some predictions for the future of AI and machine learning:

1. AI Becoming More Generalized

While current AI systems are highly specialized, future AI models will likely become more generalized. **Artificial General Intelligence (AGI)**, which refers to an AI system that can perform any intellectual task that a human can do, remains a long-term goal. Researchers believe that AGI could be achieved in the coming decades, allowing AI to perform a wide range of tasks across multiple domains.

2. AI in Creative Industries

AI is already being used in creative industries, such as music, art, and film production, to generate content, suggest creative ideas, and even compose music. In the future, AI could play a much larger role in creating original works of art, collaborating with humans to push the boundaries of creativity.

3. Increased Regulation and Ethical Guidelines

As AI systems become more integrated into society, we can expect increased **regulation** and the development of **ethical guidelines**.

Governments and organizations will need to address concerns about AI's impact on privacy, job displacement, and bias. In the coming years, regulatory bodies may introduce standards for transparency, accountability, and fairness in AI systems.

4. AI in Healthcare: A Revolution in Personalized Medicine

AI will continue to revolutionize healthcare by enabling personalized treatment plans and predicting patient outcomes with greater accuracy. **Precision medicine**, which tailors medical treatments to individual genetic profiles, will become more widespread, making healthcare more effective and less expensive.

5. AI and Sustainability

AI could play a critical role in addressing global challenges like climate change and sustainability. AI systems will be used to optimize energy usage, reduce waste, and improve resource management, helping businesses and governments reduce their environmental footprint.

Key Takeaways

- **AI is shaping the future** of technology by driving innovations in **automation**, **autonomous systems**, and **personalized experiences** across industries.

- **AI-powered automation** is transforming the workforce, with machines handling repetitive tasks while humans focus on more creative and complex jobs.

- **Autonomous systems** like self-driving cars, drones, and robots are becoming more prevalent, with AI at the heart of their functionality.

- The **intersection of AI with emerging technologies** like **blockchain**, **IoT**, and **quantum computing** is unlocking new possibilities and creating synergies between technologies.

- The **future of AI** will involve the development of **more generalized AI**, the expansion of AI's role in **creative industries**, increased **regulation**, and **sustainability efforts** to address global challenges.

In the next chapter, we will explore **AI-driven innovation**, focusing on how businesses can harness AI to drive growth, create new products, and develop strategies for the future.

CHAPTER 25

AI TOOLS AND FRAMEWORKS

In this chapter, we will explore the most popular **AI tools** and **frameworks** that are widely used by data scientists, researchers, and developers to build machine learning models. We will cover frameworks such as **TensorFlow, Keras, PyTorch**, and **scikit-learn** and help you understand how to choose the right tool for your AI project. We will also introduce cloud-based AI tools from **Google, Microsoft**, and **AWS**, and provide **hands-on examples** to demonstrate how to use these tools for practical AI development. Lastly, we will dive into a **case study** to build an AI model with **PyTorch**.

Overview of Popular AI Tools and Frameworks

There are many AI frameworks and tools available, each with its own strengths and use cases. Understanding these tools is crucial to selecting the right one for your project. Below are the most popular tools and frameworks in AI development.

1. TensorFlow

TensorFlow is an open-source framework developed by **Google** for building and deploying machine learning models. TensorFlow is widely used for deep learning and neural networks, offering extensive support for **computational graphs, parallel computing**, and **distributed training**.

- **Strengths**:
  - o Excellent support for deep learning and neural networks.
  - o Highly scalable and suitable for both research and production environments.
  - o TensorFlow has strong support for deployment, making it easy to deploy models to production environments and mobile devices.
  - o Offers a wide range of tools, such as **TensorFlow Lite** (for mobile), **TensorFlow.js** (for browser-based ML), and **TensorFlow Serving** (for model deployment).
- **Use Cases**:
  - o Image recognition
  - o Natural language processing (NLP)
  - o Time series forecasting

2. Keras

Keras is a high-level neural network API built on top of TensorFlow. It was created to provide an easy-to-use interface for building deep learning models. Keras abstracts many of the

283

complexities of TensorFlow, allowing users to quickly prototype and experiment with different model architectures.

- **Strengths**:
    - o Easy-to-use API for fast model prototyping.
    - o Great for beginners and those looking to build deep learning models with minimal setup.
    - o Now integrated directly into TensorFlow as the **default high-level API**.
- **Use Cases**:
    - o Quick prototyping of neural networks.
    - o Research and development of deep learning models.

3. PyTorch

PyTorch is an open-source machine learning framework developed by **Facebook**. It is known for its dynamic computation graph, which allows for more flexibility and easier debugging. PyTorch is widely used in academic research due to its ease of use and Pythonic design, as well as in production environments with frameworks like **TorchServe**.

- **Strengths**:
    - o Dynamic computation graph, making it easier to work with variable-length inputs and complex models.

- o Strong support for GPU acceleration.
- o Widely used in academia and research due to its simplicity and flexibility.
- o Growing adoption in production environments.
- **Use Cases**:
  - o Research and experimentation.
  - o Deep learning applications like NLP, image recognition, and reinforcement learning.

4. scikit-learn

scikit-learn is one of the most popular and accessible libraries for traditional machine learning (ML) algorithms in Python. It supports a wide range of supervised and unsupervised learning algorithms, including classification, regression, clustering, and dimensionality reduction.

- **Strengths**:
  - o Easy to use and well-documented, making it a great choice for beginners.
  - o Provides a unified interface for many popular ML algorithms.
  - o Excellent for classical machine learning tasks such as regression, classification, and clustering.
- **Use Cases**:
  - o Traditional machine learning tasks (classification, regression, clustering).

o   Feature selection and engineering.

o   Data preprocessing.

Choosing the Right Tool for Your AI Project

Choosing the right AI tool or framework depends on several factors, including the type of project, the complexity of the model, and the specific requirements of the task at hand.

1. Type of Task

- **Deep learning**: If you're building a deep learning model (e.g., image recognition, NLP, or time series forecasting), **TensorFlow** (with Keras) and **PyTorch** are the best options, as they provide the tools needed to build, train, and deploy neural networks.

- **Classical machine learning**: If your project involves more traditional machine learning algorithms (e.g., regression, classification, or clustering), **scikit-learn** is an excellent choice. It's simple to use and provides a wide range of ML algorithms out of the box.

2. Performance and Scalability

- For large-scale machine learning and deep learning models, **TensorFlow** and **PyTorch** provide better scalability and can leverage GPUs and distributed computing to speed up training.

- If your project involves deploying models on mobile devices, TensorFlow offers tools like **TensorFlow Lite** to deploy models on mobile platforms, while **TensorFlow.js** allows running models in the browser.

3. Ease of Use

- If you're new to machine learning, **Keras** (via TensorFlow) is a great starting point due to its simple API.
- **PyTorch** is favored by researchers for its flexibility and dynamic graph architecture.
- **scikit-learn** is ideal for beginners and anyone looking to apply classical machine learning techniques with ease.

Introduction to Cloud-Based AI Tools: Google AI, Microsoft Azure AI, AWS AI

In addition to traditional AI frameworks, cloud-based AI tools are becoming increasingly popular due to their scalability, ease of use, and robust infrastructure. Major cloud platforms offer a range of AI services for building, training, and deploying models.

1. Google AI

Google AI offers several services and tools for developers:

- **Google Cloud AI**: Includes **AutoML**, **TensorFlow**, and pre-trained models for tasks like image recognition, speech-to-text, and language translation.
- **Google Colab**: A free cloud-based service for running Python code with access to GPUs for training deep learning models.

2. Microsoft Azure AI

Microsoft Azure provides a suite of AI tools and services, including:

- **Azure Machine Learning**: A cloud-based service for building, training, and deploying models.
- **Azure Cognitive Services**: Pre-built APIs for tasks like vision, speech, language, and decision-making.

3. AWS AI

Amazon Web Services (AWS) offers powerful AI tools, such as:

- **AWS SageMaker**: A fully managed service for building, training, and deploying machine learning models.
- **AWS Rekognition**: Pre-trained models for image and video analysis.
- **AWS Lex**: A service for building conversational chatbots.

Hands-On Examples Using Different AI Frameworks

1. TensorFlow/Keras Example: Image Classification

Using TensorFlow (with Keras) to build a simple image classification model:

python

```python
import tensorflow as tf
from tensorflow.keras import layers, models

# Load dataset
(x_train,    y_train),    (x_test,    y_test)    =
tf.keras.datasets.cifar10.load_data()

# Preprocess the data
x_train, x_test = x_train / 255.0, x_test / 255.0

# Build the model
model = models.Sequential([
    layers.Conv2D(32, (3, 3), activation='relu',
input_shape=(32, 32, 3)),
    layers.MaxPooling2D((2, 2)),
    layers.Flatten(),
    layers.Dense(64, activation='relu'),
    layers.Dense(10, activation='softmax')
])
```

```python
# Compile the model
model.compile(optimizer='adam',
loss='sparse_categorical_crossentropy',
metrics=['accuracy'])

# Train the model
model.fit(x_train, y_train, epochs=10,
validation_data=(x_test, y_test))
```

2. PyTorch Example: Image Classification

python

```python
import torch
import torch.nn as nn
import torch.optim as optim
from torchvision import datasets, transforms

# Load dataset
transform                                       =
transforms.Compose([transforms.ToTensor(),
transforms.Normalize((0.5,), (0.5,))])
trainset    =    datasets.CIFAR10(root='./data',
train=True, download=True, transform=transform)
trainloader                                     =
torch.utils.data.DataLoader(trainset,
batch_size=4, shuffle=True)

# Define the model
class Net(nn.Module):
    def __init__(self):
```

```
        super(Net, self).__init__()
        self.conv1      =      nn.Conv2d(3,      32,
kernel_size=3, stride=1, padding=1)
        self.conv2      =      nn.Conv2d(32,      64,
kernel_size=3, stride=1, padding=1)
        self.fc1 = nn.Linear(64 * 8 * 8, 128)
        self.fc2 = nn.Linear(128, 10)


    def forward(self, x):
        x = torch.relu(self.conv1(x))
        x = torch.max_pool2d(x, 2)
        x = torch.relu(self.conv2(x))
        x = torch.max_pool2d(x, 2)
        x = x.view(-1, 64 * 8 * 8)
        x = torch.relu(self.fc1(x))
        x = self.fc2(x)
        return x


# Initialize the model, loss, and optimizer
model = Net()
criterion = nn.CrossEntropyLoss()
optimizer      =      optim.Adam(model.parameters(),
lr=0.001)


# Training loop
for epoch in range(10):
    for inputs, labels in trainloader:
        optimizer.zero_grad()
        outputs = model(inputs)
```

```
loss = criterion(outputs, labels)
loss.backward()
optimizer.step()
```

Case Study: Building an AI Model with PyTorch

Let's walk through a case study where we build a **image classifier** using **PyTorch**. We will focus on training a convolutional neural network (CNN) to classify images of **cats** and **dogs**.

Step 1: Dataset Preparation

First, we will prepare the dataset of images (e.g., the **Dogs vs Cats dataset** from Kaggle). We will use PyTorch's **DataLoader** to load and preprocess the images, ensuring they are the correct size and format for training.

Step 2: Model Architecture

We will design a simple CNN for image classification with two convolutional layers followed by fully connected layers.

Step 3: Model Training

We will train the model using an **Adam optimizer** and **cross-entropy loss**, monitoring accuracy during the training process.

Step 4: Evaluation and Testing

After training the model, we will evaluate its performance on a test set of images to assess its accuracy.

Key Takeaways

- **TensorFlow**, **Keras**, **PyTorch**, and **scikit-learn** are the most popular AI frameworks used for different types of AI tasks, from deep learning to classical machine learning.

- Choosing the right tool depends on factors like task complexity, scalability, and ease of use. **TensorFlow** and **PyTorch** are suited for deep learning tasks, while **scikit-learn** is ideal for classical machine learning.

- Cloud-based AI tools such as **Google AI**, **Microsoft Azure AI**, and **AWS AI** provide scalable infrastructure and powerful tools for building, training, and deploying AI models.

- Hands-on examples demonstrate how to use these frameworks for building AI models, with a case study on **PyTorch** showcasing how to create an image classification model.

In the next chapter, we will explore **AI ethics** and the growing need for fairness, transparency, and accountability in AI systems, particularly in real-world applications.

CHAPTER 26

BUILDING AN AI PORTFOLIO

Building a strong **AI portfolio** is a crucial step for anyone looking to break into the AI field, whether you are a beginner, an experienced developer, or someone seeking to transition into AI. A well-crafted portfolio showcases your skills, demonstrates your expertise, and can significantly improve your chances of securing job opportunities in the competitive AI job market. In this chapter, we will discuss the importance of building a strong AI portfolio, how to showcase your projects and models, the value of contributing to **open-source projects** and writing **blog posts**, and how to **build your personal brand** as an AI developer. We will also provide tips on preparing for AI job roles such as **data scientist**, **machine learning engineer**, and **AI researcher**.

The Importance of Building a Strong AI Portfolio

A well-rounded AI portfolio is more than just a collection of projects. It serves as a **reflection of your skills**, interests, and abilities, demonstrating your competence in solving real-world problems using AI techniques. It also provides tangible proof of your work, which is often more impactful than a resume alone.

1. Showcasing Practical Skills

Employers want to see practical experience, and a portfolio filled with real-world AI projects can show them that you can solve complex problems, understand data science concepts, and apply machine learning algorithms effectively.

2. Demonstrating Problem-Solving Abilities

Building a portfolio gives you the opportunity to showcase your ability to approach and solve problems. By working on diverse projects and applying different AI techniques, you can highlight how you address challenges and implement solutions.

3. Standing Out in the Job Market

In the competitive field of AI, a strong portfolio helps differentiate you from other candidates. It acts as proof that you not only have theoretical knowledge but can also apply it effectively to practical challenges.

Showcasing Your AI Projects and Models

To create a portfolio that stands out, you should carefully select and present your **AI projects**. Each project should showcase different aspects of your skill set, from data collection and cleaning to model training and deployment.

1. Project Selection

Select a diverse set of projects that demonstrate a range of techniques, such as:

- **Supervised Learning**: Regression and classification tasks.
- **Unsupervised Learning**: Clustering and anomaly detection.
- **Deep Learning**: Image classification, natural language processing (NLP), or reinforcement learning.
- **End-to-End Projects**: Projects where you handle everything from data collection and cleaning to model deployment.

2. Code Repositories

Host your code on a public repository such as **GitHub** or **GitLab**. This allows potential employers or collaborators to view your work and contribute if needed. Organize your repositories clearly, with detailed README files explaining the project, your approach, and how to run the code.

3. Model Deployment

Where possible, deploy your models as **APIs** or **web applications** so that others can interact with them. Use platforms like **Heroku**, **AWS**, or **Google Cloud** to deploy models, or use **Flask** and

FastAPI for building lightweight APIs. Deploying a model in production is a key skill that employers will value.

4. Visualizations

Use data visualizations and model performance graphs to explain the results of your projects. This helps employers quickly understand how you approached the problem and how well the model performs. Tools like **Matplotlib**, **Seaborn**, and **Plotly** can be used to create high-quality visualizations.

Writing Blog Posts and Contributing to Open-Source Projects

One of the best ways to build your **AI portfolio** is by sharing your knowledge and contributing to the AI community. Writing blog posts and participating in open-source projects can enhance your visibility and credibility in the field.

1. Writing Blog Posts

- **Explain Complex Topics**: Write blog posts that break down complex AI topics, such as **neural networks**, **reinforcement learning**, or **model evaluation techniques**, into simple, digestible content. This demonstrates your ability to communicate technical concepts effectively.

- **Share Your Projects**: Document your AI projects in detail, explaining the problem, the data you worked with, your model choice, and the results. Provide code snippets and share insights into the challenges you faced and how you overcame them.
- **Teach Through Tutorials**: Create step-by-step tutorials that help others learn. For instance, you can guide readers through building a simple **image classification model** with **TensorFlow**, or a **sentiment analysis model** using **scikit-learn**.

Platforms to Publish:

- **Medium**: Popular platform for publishing technical blogs and tutorials.
- **Dev.to**: A developer-focused community where you can write and share content.
- **Personal Blog**: Consider starting a personal blog with platforms like **WordPress** or **Hugo** to establish your online presence.

2. Contributing to Open-Source Projects

Contributing to open-source AI projects is a great way to gain real-world experience, collaborate with other developers, and improve your code. Some well-known open-source projects in the AI space include:

- **TensorFlow**: Google's open-source deep learning framework.
- **PyTorch**: A flexible deep learning framework from Facebook.
- **scikit-learn**: A popular library for classical machine learning algorithms.

You can start by contributing small fixes, bug reports, or enhancements, and gradually work your way up to larger contributions.

Building a Personal Brand as an AI Developer

In today's competitive job market, building a **personal brand** is essential for standing out. This involves establishing your presence and reputation as an AI developer, both online and offline.

1. Social Media Presence

- **LinkedIn**: Regularly update your profile with your AI projects, skills, and certifications. Join AI-related groups, participate in discussions, and connect with professionals in the field.
- **Twitter**: Follow AI researchers, companies, and other developers to stay up to date with industry trends. Share

your projects, blog posts, and insights to increase your visibility.

- **GitHub**: Share your work on GitHub and maintain a consistent activity log to showcase your contributions to AI projects.

2. Networking

Attend AI conferences, webinars, and meetups to connect with like-minded professionals and expand your network. Participate in hackathons, both online and offline, to build relationships with other developers and gain hands-on experience.

3. AI Certifications

Certifications from recognized platforms like **Coursera**, **edX**, or **Udacity** can boost your credentials and demonstrate your commitment to continuous learning. Popular AI certifications include:

- **TensorFlow Developer Certificate**: Offered by Google for those proficient in TensorFlow.
- **Microsoft Azure AI Engineer Associate**: Certification for those working with AI solutions on Azure.
- **AWS Certified Machine Learning – Specialty**: A certification focused on deploying machine learning models on AWS.

Preparing for AI Job Roles: Data Scientist, Machine Learning Engineer, AI Researcher

Your portfolio, combined with experience and certifications, will help you prepare for various AI roles. Below are the key roles and how to prepare for them:

1. Data Scientist

- **Key Skills**: Statistical analysis, data manipulation, machine learning, and data visualization.
- **Portfolio Focus**: Highlight projects that involve analyzing complex datasets, building predictive models, and communicating insights using visualizations.

2. Machine Learning Engineer

- **Key Skills**: Proficiency in machine learning algorithms, software development, and model deployment.
- **Portfolio Focus**: Show projects where you have built and deployed machine learning models. Emphasize **model optimization, scalability**, and **production-readiness**.

3. AI Researcher

- **Key Skills**: Advanced knowledge of AI theory, mathematical modeling, and research methodologies.

- **Portfolio Focus**: Showcase any research papers, contributions to AI conferences, and complex AI models. Having a deep understanding of **theoretical AI** and **cutting-edge technologies** will be essential for this role.

Key Takeaways

- **Building a strong AI portfolio** is crucial for showcasing your skills, attracting potential employers, and standing out in the job market.
- **Showcase your projects** by selecting diverse, real-world tasks and deploying models to production where possible. Use GitHub to share code and build a strong online presence.
- **Writing blog posts** and **contributing to open-source projects** helps establish your expertise and contribute to the AI community.
- **Building a personal brand** through social media, networking, and certifications can elevate your visibility and credibility in the AI field.
- **Prepare for AI job roles** by tailoring your portfolio to highlight the key skills needed for positions like **data scientist**, **machine learning engineer**, or **AI researcher**.

In the next chapter, we will explore **AI ethics and governance**, discussing the growing importance of responsible AI development and deployment in today's world.

CHAPTER 27

CONCLUSION AND NEXT STEPS

Congratulations on completing this comprehensive guide to **Artificial Intelligence (AI)**! In this final chapter, we will recap the key concepts you've learned throughout the book, provide suggestions for continuing your AI journey, and offer guidance on preparing for an AI career. Whether you're just starting out or are well on your way to becoming an AI expert, there are always new opportunities to grow and contribute to the ever-evolving field of AI.

Recap of What You've Learned Throughout the Book

Throughout this book, you've gained a deep understanding of AI, from the foundational concepts to advanced techniques. Here's a quick summary of the key topics we covered:

- **Introduction to AI**: You learned about AI's fundamental concepts, its history, and its applications across various industries.
- **Machine Learning Basics**: You explored different types of machine learning algorithms, including supervised,

unsupervised, and reinforcement learning, as well as key techniques like classification, regression, and clustering.

- **Deep Learning and Neural Networks**: We delved into deep learning techniques, including convolutional neural networks (CNNs) for image recognition and recurrent neural networks (RNNs) for sequential data tasks.

- **AI Tools and Frameworks**: You were introduced to popular AI frameworks like **TensorFlow**, **Keras**, **PyTorch**, and **scikit-learn**, and learned how to choose the right tool for different AI tasks.

- **AI Applications**: You explored the application of AI in various industries, such as healthcare, finance, retail, and autonomous systems, and learned how AI is transforming business and industry.

- **AI Development Challenges**: We discussed the common challenges in AI development, including data quality, scaling models, model drift, and deployment issues.

- **AI Ethics and Fairness**: You learned about the importance of addressing bias, ensuring fairness, and protecting privacy in AI systems.

- **Building an AI Portfolio**: We covered how to showcase your skills through a well-rounded AI portfolio, contribute to open-source projects, and build your personal brand in the AI community.

Continuing Your AI Journey: Further Reading and Resources

AI is a vast field, and there is always more to learn. To continue your journey, consider diving deeper into the following areas:

1. Online Courses and Specializations

- **Coursera**: Offers numerous AI and machine learning courses, including the **AI Specialization by Andrew Ng** and the **Deep Learning Specialization**.
- **edX**: Provides a range of AI-related courses, such as the **Artificial Intelligence (AI) MicroMasters Program** from Columbia University.
- **Udacity**: Offers AI-focused **nanodegrees**, including programs on deep learning, AI for robotics, and AI in business.

2. Books

- **"Hands-On Machine Learning with Scikit-Learn, Keras, and TensorFlow"** by Aurélien Géron: A practical guide to building machine learning models using Python.
- **"Deep Learning"** by Ian Goodfellow, Yoshua Bengio, and Aaron Courville: A foundational book for anyone interested in deep learning.
- **"Pattern Recognition and Machine Learning"** by Christopher Bishop: A comprehensive textbook on statistical machine learning and pattern recognition.

3. Research Papers and Journals

- Stay updated with the latest research by reading papers from top AI conferences like **NeurIPS**, **ICML**, and **CVPR**. Websites like **arXiv.org** offer free access to cutting-edge research papers in AI and machine learning.

4. YouTube Channels and Podcasts

- **Siraj Raval**: A YouTube channel that provides fun and engaging tutorials on AI and machine learning.
- **Lex Fridman Podcast**: Features in-depth interviews with leading experts in AI, robotics, and technology.
- **Data Skeptic**: A podcast that discusses machine learning, AI, and data science in a digestible format.

Joining AI Communities and Contributing to the Field

One of the best ways to accelerate your learning and make connections in the AI field is by joining AI communities. These communities provide a space for learning, sharing knowledge, and collaborating on projects.

1. Online Communities

- **Kaggle**: A platform for data science competitions where you can practice your skills on real-world datasets and learn from the global community.
- **Stack Overflow**: Engage with other developers to ask questions, provide answers, and share knowledge on AI and programming.
- **AI Subreddits**: Communities like **r/MachineLearning** and **r/learnmachinelearning** are great for discussing AI trends, sharing resources, and getting advice.

2. Meetups and Conferences

- Attend AI-related meetups, conferences, and hackathons to network with industry professionals, learn about the latest trends, and collaborate on exciting projects.
- Popular conferences include **NeurIPS**, **ICML**, **CVPR**, and **AAAI**.

3. Open-Source Contributions

- Contribute to **open-source AI projects** by working on codebases, writing documentation, fixing bugs, or improving existing models. GitHub is a great place to find AI projects that need contributors.

Contributing to these communities will not only help you learn more but also allow you to give back to the field, establish yourself as a thought leader, and grow your professional network.

Preparing for an AI Career: Building Your Skills and Network

As you continue your AI journey, it's essential to develop the skills and network that will help you thrive in the competitive job market.

1. Building Your Skills

- **Master the Basics**: Ensure you have a solid understanding of **mathematics, statistics, probability**, and **linear algebra**. These are crucial for understanding machine learning algorithms and models.
- **Programming**: Be proficient in **Python**, the primary language for AI development. Learn libraries such as **NumPy**, **Pandas**, and **Matplotlib** for data manipulation and visualization.
- **ML Frameworks**: Gain hands-on experience with AI frameworks like **TensorFlow**, **PyTorch**, **scikit-learn**, and **Keras**. Learn how to train, evaluate, and deploy models using these tools.

2. Networking

- Connect with **AI professionals** on LinkedIn and join relevant AI groups.
- Attend **meetups**, **conferences**, and **webinars** to network with like-minded individuals and potential employers.
- Reach out to AI experts and ask for mentorship or advice. Building relationships with industry professionals can provide valuable insights into the field and potential job opportunities.

3. Job Roles in AI

The AI field offers a wide range of career opportunities, including:

- **Data Scientist**: Focuses on analyzing data, building predictive models, and extracting actionable insights.
- **Machine Learning Engineer**: Specializes in designing, building, and deploying machine learning models and systems.
- **AI Researcher**: Works on advancing the theoretical understanding of AI, developing new algorithms, and contributing to AI literature.
- **AI Product Manager**: Focuses on driving AI products from conception to execution, collaborating with engineers, data scientists, and business teams.

As you build your portfolio and skills, tailor your job applications to highlight your expertise in AI and machine learning. Ensure your portfolio includes relevant projects and that your resume emphasizes your hands-on experience and problem-solving abilities.

Final Thoughts and Encouragement for Future AI Developers

The field of **Artificial Intelligence** is vast, exciting, and filled with endless opportunities. Whether you're interested in applying AI to solve real-world problems, advancing AI research, or developing cutting-edge applications, there is a place for you in this dynamic field.

Remember that the journey to becoming an AI expert is continuous. Technologies evolve, new research emerges, and challenges are ever-present. The key to success is **curiosity**, **dedication**, and **collaboration**. Stay updated, never stop learning, and most importantly, be persistent.

AI has the power to revolutionize industries, change lives, and shape the future, and you are now part of this transformation. Keep experimenting, contributing, and building, and you will have the opportunity to make a significant impact.

Best of luck in your AI journey, and keep pushing the boundaries of what is possible with AI!

Key Takeaways

- Building a strong AI portfolio is essential for showcasing your skills, demonstrating your expertise, and standing out in the job market.
- **Contribute to the community** by writing blogs, engaging in open-source projects, and sharing your knowledge.
- **Prepare for an AI career** by building your skills, gaining hands-on experience, and networking with other professionals in the field.
- AI is a rapidly evolving field, and continuous learning, curiosity, and perseverance are key to succeeding.

In your next steps, keep honing your skills, embrace new opportunities, and contribute to the AI community. The future of AI is bright, and you are part of that future.

Printed in Great Britain
by Amazon